I
See
Jesus

Rev. Alfred L. Decker

ISBN 979-8-89345-503-8 (paperback)
ISBN 979-8-89345-504-5 (digital)

Christian Faith Publishing
832 Park Avenue
Meadville, PA 16335
www.christianfaithpublishing.com

Printed in the United States of America

Contents

List of Scriptures

Psalm 23:1–6
Psalm 34:1–3
Psalm 56:11
Isaiah 41:10
Matthew 5:11–12
Matthew 5:44–45
Matthew 6:21
Matthew 12:36–37
Matthew 18:22
Matthew 19:14
Luke 10:21
Luke 11:11–13
Luke 23:32–43
John 5:24
John 10:10
John 15:11
John 17:11–12, 15
Acts 17:28
Romans 8:1
Romans 8:27–28
Romans 8:35, 37, 38
1 Corinthians 13:11–12
2 Corinthians 5:17
Galatians 5:22–23
Ephesians 6:1
Colossians 3:17
1 John 3:1
1 John 5:12
Revelation 7:9

Preface

The entire Bible is God's inspired Word. From the first word of Genesis to the last word of Revelation, every word is revealing the love of God through Jesus Christ and the Holy Spirit. Near the center of the Holy Bible is the most widely known scripture in history: the Twenty-Third Psalm. This work of King David tells us about Jesus.

This work uses the general progression of David's psalm to provide a format familiar to us. This is a blending of real-life events, poetry, and one fictional work. May you discover the presence of Jesus in your life.

Acknowledgments

Jesus Christ is our Lord and Savior. He is the Son of God, the Living Word of all creation. Jesus is the Son of Man, the one with the authority to bear our sins at Calvary, who was raised from death by God, who willingly gave up his glory to bear the scars on his body for our salvation. He is our creator, sustainer, and promised future. To him belongs our praise, our lives, and our eternity.

What we are about to read are stories about Jesus as he dealt with those who were involved with my life. Isn't it true that Jesus is the author of all life? Didn't he form us in the womb? Don't we possess the very "breath" of God himself? *This is a book about Jesus.* Take the life of any person and allow yourself to see God working in that life. *Jesus is Lord and Savior.*

Everything in this book is real and factual. There are no fictional people. No one is a composite of different characters. In a few cases, I used a different name to protect a real name. Those times are clearly stated. All quotations are reported to the best of my ability.

I have been blessed with many friends and family members who encouraged me to write this book:

Chuck and Becky McCoskey, who encouraged, cajoled, and threatened to keep me writing.

Josh, Julie, and Kaitlyn Woodall, who always read everything I wrote.

Linda Ridlen, my cousin, who always had time to discuss my progress.

I thank God, Jesus, and the Holy Spirit above all others.

Remember, this is a book about God, Jesus, and the Holy Spirit. May you see Jesus working in your own life.

Introduction

"I see Jesus." Three words that change everything and everyone. Jesus is the Son of God. Jesus is our Lord. Jesus is the Messiah. In him, we live and move. He is our light and our resurrection. He *is* God, and he *is* the Holy Spirit.

He gave up his glory to become a human. He chose ordinary people to become his disciples. They told the world about Jesus. Generation after generation continued to follow Jesus. From thirteen to billions, in less than two thousand years. How many have seen Jesus? That number is unknown.

What we do know is the fact that Jesus is real, and he is in heaven working for us. We also know that everyone who does see Jesus has their lives changed. Those who accept the love of Jesus may not have a vision of Jesus, but they see Jesus with eyes of faith.

It is faith that leads us to Jesus. It is faith that urges us to believe in Jesus. Once we accept Jesus as our Savior, we join the hosts of heaven as we declare, "I see Jesus."

The purpose of this book is to help us see Jesus in our daily lives. We may be at work, at home, on a vacation, or in the grocery store, Jesus is there. Be it noon or midnight, Jesus is there. May the poetry focus us on the divinity of Jesus, as the stories open our minds to Jesus's daily presence in our lives.

Diane Decker
My eternal love
in Christ Jesus.

Chapter 1

I See Jesus

Psalm 34:1–3
> I will bless the Lord at all times;
> his praise will always be on my lips.
> I will boast in the Lord;
> the humble will hear and be glad.
> Proclaim the Lord's greatness with me;
> let us exalt his name together.

I See Jesus

This is the true story of Diane Decker's final days on this earth. She was born on December 22, 1954. She was a beautiful baby who grew into a beautiful young woman. We met in 1972 at a church-sponsored youth camp. A group of teenagers were taking turns standing in the middle of a circle. Each person would ask a question for the other teens to answer.

I was walking past and decided to see why everyone was in the circle. I squeezed into the crowd and saw Diane. I immediately fell in love with her! There stood the girl of my dreams! She was gorgeous! She asked if she should do her homework first or read the Bible. I responded, "Read the Bible first!" That made her look at me, and as the old saying goes, lightning struck. She accepted my proposal on our second date. We were married on December 28, 1974.

Time passed until 2017. That was the year Diane's health took a turn for the worse. Most of that year was spent going to doctors and hospitals. Her health was rapidly declining. We finally went to a major hospital in Indianapolis. They said she needed a liver transplant, but her health kept declining. After a month in ICU, a large team of doctors and nurses gathered in her hospital room. They told us she should go home to hospice care. They stood there with their heads bowed, and everyone was crying. They had grown attached to Diane. A few hours later, two nurses helped me put Diane into our van for the ride home. They were openly weeping as I pulled away from the hospital.

Their final instructions were to allow Diane anything she wanted to eat and drink. All she wanted was a hamburger with a giant orange drink!

The hospice people were waiting for us at our house. We set up a hospital bed, with other equipment, in the living room. Diane could watch television while being near me and our Pomeranian named Baby Doll. Her strength was quickly diminishing. She could barely move, and she spoke in a soft whisper.

On September 10, she said to me, "I want to tell you something."

Leaning close, I said, "Yes, Diane."

"I have three more days to live," she spoke calmly, as if she was a reporter.

"Okay," was all I could say. How was I supposed to respond to such a statement? There was no room for debate. She had been given a fixed time. Her next statement was almost too much to hear.

"I want to stay with you. I am going to miss you."

I wanted her to think I was strong, her rock, willing and able to help her face her passing. I failed. I wept that she was about to die. I wept because I was going to miss her. I wept because she loved me. Such love!

I said, "Honey, it's okay. There is no time in heaven. You will be worshipping Jesus, and when you turn around, I will be standing there!"

She was quiet for a few minutes. She appeared to be pondering what I told her.

A few minutes later, she spoke in a calm voice. "I see Jesus, and he's standing there, smiling and motioning for me to join him."

I was amazed! She had seen our Lord! I was in awe of Diane. She could see into the beyond!

"The next time you see him, go to him."

With that, she drifted off to sleep.

Three days later, she whispered, "I have to tell you something."

I suddenly knew what she was going to say. "Yes, dear?"

"I see Jesus. There are a bunch of people with him. They are all smiling and motioning for me to join them."

Tears were going down my cheeks. I wanted so much to hold on to her, to keep her for myself. I couldn't do that to her. I had to release her to God.

"It's okay to go. I love you."

Her eyes closed. She was still breathing. I watched her closely. She was sleeping. A few minutes passed. Everything was very quiet. There was no noise in the neighborhood. The dog was totally still.

It was 9:22 a.m. That was the moment I knew Diane had stepped into heaven. Then I noticed her left hand. Her fingers were wrapped around the top of one of the safety rails, with her arm reaching upward.

Her last action was to reach up to Jesus!

I wept then, and I weep now.

My heartache is heaven's rejoicing.

We will be together again.

We will spend eternity rejoicing in the love of Jesus Christ, our Lord and God!

Will you be there with us? Have you asked Jesus to take away your sins? Will you be another person who sees Jesus? He loves you!

(September 5, 2023)

The Glory of Jesus

There is one thought that brings me pleasure,
When I am living in Heaven forever.
I will see Jesus my wonderful Savior.
Such glory and majesty, he is my treasure!

Then the thought occurred to me,
Why must I wait to see his radiance?
The Holy Spirit gives us guidance.
In the Bible the glory of Jesus we see!

Peter, James, and John saw the Transfiguration.
To meet with Moses and Elijah, he was Glorified!
His face was brighter than the sun. His robe was whiter than light!
Jesus is the glory of every nation!

Then John had a revelation of Jesus glorified.
His hair was pure white, his eyes like fire so bright.
His face shone like the sun; his feet glowed like pure bronze.
He wore a golden sash, his voice as powerful as the raging sea.

Jesus is glorified by God for eternity.
He is the Light of God, given for you and me.
We must confess our sins and ask Jesus to live within.
Only Jesus's love can save us, a love freely given!

(December 27, 2022)

My Shepherd

David wrote, "The Lord is my shepherd," in Psalm Twenty-Three,
In John chapter 10, Jesus said again, "I am the good shepherd,
I know my sheep and my sheep know me."

God's Son is our Shepherd, he tends to our care,
We know that he loves us, yet we are all unique.
We understand his love, it's the "how" and "when" we seek,
Look at John chapter 10, our truth is written there.

Jesus spoke about himself, "I tell you the truth,
He calls his own sheep by name and leads them out,
He goes on ahead of them, and his sheep follow him,
The thief comes to steal, kill, and destroy.
I have come that they may have life and have it to the full.

I have other sheep that are not of this pen
They will listen to my voice; I must bring them also.
My Father loves me. I lay down my life—only to take it up again.
This command I received from my Father.
I have authority to lay it down, and take it up again"

"The Lord is my shepherd," the words are easily spoken.
Do we mean them from the heart, or just as a token?
Examine your soul, look deep inside,
Is Jesus really your shepherd? Are you truly alive?

Jesus is your answer, always taking care of you.
His blood was shed at Calvary, he left an empty tomb,
Our Risen Savior calls us, Jesus is calling you!
Ask for his forgiveness. Jesus is your Good Shepherd, too.

(November 18, 2022)

Thank You, Jesus

Thank you, Jesus; thank you, O Lord.
We give you the praise your Greatness deserves.
Rejoice in your Glory, we tell your story.
We thank you and praise you as we observe:

Who walked on water, who calmed the sea?
Who cast out demons, who raised the dead?
Who healed lepers, who made the blind see?
Who made the lame man carry his bed?

Who was betrayed for you and for me?
Who hung on a cross, who took our sin?
Who gave up his life at Calvary?
Who rose from the tomb and lives again?

Thank you, Jesus; thank you, Oh, Lord
We give you the praise you so richly deserve.
We praise you! We love you! You we adore!
Our Savior, Redeemer, God's Living Word.

Here we are Jesus, here is our love,
Teach us, mold us, make us like you.
We give praise to the Lamb of God,
Thank you, Jesus! We love you!

(November 11, 2022)

Love Me

Jesus told the story of two men who lived long ago.
One man was rich, his wealth amazing to behold.
The other was named Lazarus: poor, ill, and all alone.
He sat in despair outside of the rich man's home.

The rich man enjoyed what the world could offer.
Fame, power, authority; he did not suffer.
While at his door sat a poor, wretched man.
No fame, no power, he loved God, the Great I Am.

The rich man died and found himself in Hell.
A life of selfishness and pride was all he could tell.
He had rejected God's love, now he was undone.
It was too late to repent, an eternity without God's Son.

Lazarus also died; his broken body left on the ground.
All for him was light, and joy was all around!
He had a perfect body. Abraham and God were with him.
His joy overflowed as he praised God with hymns!

Today the choice is ours, whose will we be?
Will we serve ourselves or those in need?
Will we repent to Jesus and ask him to forgive?
Will we reject him for our own way of life?

God's love never changes. Jesus died for all.
His love is eternal and sufficient. Jesus is all in all.
Give your life, soul, and heart to Jesus's love.
Lord, love me like I don't deserve; love me with your Love!

(July 1, 2023)

Like Jesus

I want to be like Jesus, my One and Only Lord,
I want to be like Jesus, To him I will be true.
He is my inspiration, God's Holy Living Word,
I want to love like Jesus, I want to see you.

Oh, the glory of your splendor, the glory that is you!
What will it be like, when you I finally see?
The only scars that I see, are carried by you,
There is no thought of me, when Jesus I see.

It is in you, Lord, that I am complete,
The love you shared at Calvary, will truly make me whole.
You are the Lamb of God, death you did defeat,
The joy inside me! You have saved my very soul!

Help me, Lord, to be more like you.
Let others see you in me, like I see me in you!
Salvation, forgiveness, compassion and love,
Heaven on earth and Heaven above.

Here is my heart Lord, all that I am,
The good, the bad, the happy and sad.
From confusion to confidence, in you I am,
I want to be like Jesus, in him I will be glad!

(November 21, 2022)

No Pretending

If we say that we are saved, that Jesus makes us whole,
Then the question must be asked, what about my soul?
There are people in distress, who call on Jesus's Name,
They offer him their body, but do not give him their soul.

These people have seen a great light, but still live in the night.
They say, here am I take me, but not my soul.
Giving the body alone is like flying a plane without engines.
The passengers and crew say, "Vroom, Vroom," it's just pretending!

Jesus died and rose again; on him we can depend!
When Jesus hung on that old rugged cross,
He gave God his body and his soul.
His was a complete sacrifice, Jesus gave his all.

"Father, into your hands I commit my spirit,"
Jesus cried out with a loud voice.
With this said, he breathed his last.
Jesus set our example, what it means to be whole.

Our love for Jesus must be complete.
To offer our body, but not the soul, ends in defeat.
When we give Jesus our soul, then we will know,
The victory of salvation is giving God our
soul, giving him total control.

(December 26, 2022)

Choose This Day

This is the first day of a new year,
Time to consider what was and will be.
There were times of laughter and tears,
Quiet times and times of activity.

God calls to us with his loving heart,
He is forever and always the same.
Always ready to give us a new start,
Ready to forgive our sins and shame.

How do we honor God on this first day?
Will it be spent in a drunken stupor?
Or dazed by a drug? A high price to pay!
Or locked in a cell by a trooper?

There is a much better way,
One that pleases our Holy Lord.
Start with prayer on that first day,
And time to read God's Word.

Turn our hearts to God's only Son.
Focus our minds on the Mind of Christ.
Not my will, but yours be done!
Melt the frozen heart of sinful ice.

See us, Jesus, as we truly are.
We bow before you this first day,
Save us, Lord, live in our hearts.
Lead us on your Holy Way!

I SEE JESUS

Time goes by, the first day has gone.
Another day written in our history.
May every day find us pleasing God's Son.
Yes, Jesus loves you and me!

(January 2, 2024)

The Longest Ride, Ever

Some events are remembered with humor; some with sadness; and some with a mixture of both. Of course, a memory is affected by the intensity of the experience. The more intense the emotional effect, the deeper the memory. There is the opposite possible reaction too. An intense event may lead to the loss of a memory. We are blessed by God to have memories.

It would be in our best interests to take our memories to God in prayer. Every memory is a gift if we allow God to have control of the memory. He can turn a painful memory into a peaceful memory, just as he can take a sad memory and make it a joyful memory.

It was June of 1972. Diane, my future wife, and I attended Anderson College, now called Anderson University. We were looking for a ride back to Pennsylvania when Reverend and Mrs. R. agreed to take us back home. The only stipulation was a side trip to see a new bridge a few miles off the road.

Indiana had beautiful weather while Pennsylvania had heavy rain. The rain was caused by a large storm covering the entire central part of the state. The storm was stationary for three days, soaking the soil and raising water levels.

In the Atlantic Ocean, Hurricane Agnes formed. Three days of rain from the first storm ended just before Agnes arrived with incredible rain. Agnes produced eight to fifteen inches of rain per day for another three to four days.

When we started for Pennsylvania, we had planned on reaching our homes within eight hours. Our hosts were very sweet people. We always enjoyed talking with them. The trip started after a prayer for travelling mercy and quickly changed into the longest ride, ever!

By the time we started our trip, the storm was all over the news. Pastor R. was driving. The radio was on a music channel, playing softly so we could talk. Both Diane and I had to use a bus service for previous trips, so we knew they stopped everywhere, making a six-hour trip in ten hours. We soon discovered that we were experiencing the same thing in a car!

Not only did we drive slowly, but we also kept making stops. Remember, we were college students. We liked to drive fast. Without speaking, we had a conversation with lip reading and subtle motions.

DIANE: How long?

ME: I don't know!

DIANE: Well?

ME: Well, what?

DIANE: Say something!

I brought up the subject by asking how long it would take until we would get to the new bridge. Pastor R. said it wouldn't be long. Now, I am going to be very honest, I really felt like starting the ritual "Are we there yet?" I just kept quiet and tolerated the slow pace. We finally reached the bridge, which was very impressive in 1972. What caught our attention was the height of the river. The water was almost over the deck of the old bridge. That, along with the news on the radio, prompted him to pick up the pace to get us home before the heavy rain started.

We managed to get home before the worst of the storm. Reverend and Mrs. R. went to Jersey Shore, Pennsylvania. I took Diane to the intersection of Interstate 80 and the Northeast Extension of the Pennsylvania Turnpike, where her parents picked her up.

Agnes was such a large storm that the weather service retired the name afterward. Every state from Florida to New York, Pennsylvania and Ohio suffered from the storm. In Jersey Shore, the river crested at 38.4 feet! That was eleven feet above the historical level. I lived one-fourth of a mile from the river. The rescue crews docked their boats in front of our building!

In Pittsburgh, the Ohio River crested at 25.82 feet. Philadelphia had local flooding, and millions of dollars in damage. In Harrisburg, 15 percent of the city was underwater as hundreds of homes burned down, leaving five thousand homeless. Lancaster County, southeast of Harrisburg, had fifteen destroyed bridges. Finally, Wilkes-Berra had to evacuate one hundred thousand people.

The devastation was the worst in Pennsylvania's history. The total damage exceeded two billion dollars. How should we view such tragic events? Is God judging people? Has he set nature in motion and keeps "hands off"?

Are we to be concerned about others who suffer from such events? When we started this trip, Diane and I were only concerned about ourselves. Reverend R. had three other lives to be thinking about. He chose to drive safely. His love and concern for Diane and I was far better than we had for him and Mrs. R. Everyone has times when they are selfish.

Christians must deal with life as they believe Jesus leads them. We must not turn a blind eye to the truth as revealed by God. *Being selfish not only leads us to minimize what others feel, it will eventually harden our own hearts and lead us into isolation. Isolation most likely will lead to rejecting God, risking an eternity in hell.*

Jesus Christ set the example for us as recorded in the Bible. The apostles followed his example, proving average people can live like Jesus. We have two thousand years of people living like Jesus. Why should we be any different? God is still God. Jesus is still Jesus. The Holy Spirit is still the Holy Spirit.

What we do for others is the most important criteria at the great judgment (Matthew 25:40). God wants us to love others. When people suffer from tragedy, we must love them as God gives us opportunity. When people are caught in a cycle of selfishness, it is our opportunity to help them find the freedom of Christ.

The longest ride—ever? It wasn't a trip to Pennsylvania. It is the ride we call life. Life is the eternal ride. Life never ends. Our souls are eternal. Are we on the ride to hell or heaven? What about people we know? What is their ultimate destination?

May we choose to live with Jesus!

Thank you for loving me, Father. I choose you and Jesus to live with me for all eternity. Help me to love others as you love me. In Jesus's name, Amen.

(June 5, 2023)

A Worthy Life

The Kingdom of God is filled with those who believe.
Their stories are different; yet the same.
Whatever their struggle, they found faith on their knees.
They relied on Jesus to redeem their pain.

Our struggles are real, with suffering and agony.
God understands all that we truly need.
God wants the very best for you and me.
The way we accept his Will, is the way we accept his Victory!

"Faith is being sure of what we hope for,
And certain of what we do not see."
Ours is a living faith, always doing more.
Gladly accepting whatever God asks us to be.

Our love for Jesus must be alive,
Not just some dead theology.
We must do more than just survive.
People must see Jesus in you and me!

When the times of trial are upon us,
When we are tempted to just surrender,
Remember! We serve Jesus, the Victorious!
All fear, doubt, worry and sin; he has torn asunder!

God the Father calls us his children.
Let us live each day like Jesus.
What we do to others we do to him.
Our lives must point to salvation in Jesus!

REV. ALFRED L. DECKER

Ours is a life of service to our King.
Our goal is to show people Jesus's love.
Be strong and faithful in everything.
May our lives be our worship! Praise God above!

(February 17, 2023)

My Choice

God is our Father, our Creator is he, call
him Abba or call him Daddy.
His great love is all we need. So, what is the matter with me?
All was perfect with Adam and Eve; Eden was Heaven on earth.
They walked with God in his handiwork.
So, what is the matter with me?

I love the Lord, I really do! I go to church to pray and sing.
I listen to the sermon, too. Honestly, it doesn't mean a thing.
Whatever happened to my joy? Where has my excitement gone?
What can I do to be restored? Please, tell me, what is wrong?

Let me tell you, God heard my cry, his answer was just for me.
I am still with you, look deep inside.
I did not leave you, you left me!
I give everyone my only Son. I call him Jesus; you call him Lord.
My love for you is never done. Listen now, I will be heard.

I know your thoughts; I know your heart.
I knew you before you were born.
I will save you and give you a new start.
It's done through Jesus your Lord.
He gave his life at Calvary; he left an empty tomb.
He gave you our Holy Spirit. The rest is up to you.

My love is yours for asking. My love is forever true.
Ask Jesus to be your King, that is all you need to do.
Tell Jesus all your sins. Surrender all to him.
His blood will change all you've been.
His love will make you born again.

Now, put my Love that's in your heart,
in service to others in my name.
The more you serve, the more you gain
as my joy and love fill your heart.
I am Father, yes, that is Me. Call me Abba or Daddy, too.
I am all you will ever need. There is nothing the matter with you!

You are my child; it is you I love.
I am always with you. I cherish you!
To your love and worship, I say well done!
You are a blessing to me! Yes, you!

(December 8, 2022)

School Life

It has been said that everything I needed to learn I learned in grade school. I learned many things in all the grade levels. I may not remember the teachers' names, but I remember their personalities. The following memories either happened to me or I was affected by the actions of other people. Are you ready to go to school? Let's go!

My school years were very different from today. We did not have cell phones. No backpacks. No calculators. We were given our textbooks and had to return them at the end of the year. Teacher supplies were provided by the schools. If you lived in town, you walked or rode a bicycle to school. Discipline worked up to spanking. If that failed, you were suspended up to being expelled. You respected the teachers, never yelled in the hallways, and dreaded the principal. If you didn't have lunch money or didn't bring lunch, you didn't eat. After-school activities had similar rules.

One day, in grade school, another boy stabbed a girl's hand with a pencil. When the teacher returned to the room, the kids said I did it! I claimed my innocence to her and the principal. What I said didn't matter. They knew I was guilty. My parents would be notified, and they would discuss my suspension. The teacher and I returned to a completely silent room. I felt everyone staring at me. That was the moment a boy stood up and confessed to stabbing the girl. I felt relief, and I expected an apology. I never got an apology. Instead, the teacher said I was lucky, and she was going to keep an eye on me.

There was another elementary teacher who was an older woman who had a genuine love for her students. I have no idea what she taught; I just remember her kindness, patience and love.

I recall one more teacher. She was firm, but patient, with her students. She taught us to read and write. I remember the paper with three oversized lines that we used to shape our letters. My favorite letter was the *O*. She gave me the ability to read and write. I don't remember her name. I will always be grateful for her.

Elementary school taught me about life. Then came junior high school. Buckle your seat belts, the ride is going to get very rough.

The years of junior high wouldn't be bad if physical development matched emotional development. I worked hard to keep a low profile. The things I remember about those years involved the teachers and my dad.

The geography teacher was a man easily remembered. He was the last one into the room on the first day. He did it for dramatic effect. He towered over us at seven feet eight inches tall! Then he held up his foot to show his size 15 shoe. He pointed to a shoeprint on the wall and told us he would kick us as punishment! His wife and two children also stood over seven feet tall. One time, a student was kicked by the teacher. He stood the rest of the day!

Our school was a three-story building that served the town for theatrical productions. Our assembly hall had a main floor with two large balconies. The floors of all three areas sloped downward to the main stage. The school occupied the area encircling the auditorium. The auditorium could seat over six hundred people.

My dad was one of the custodians. He would do anything required by his job. He also had epilepsy. One Saturday I went with Dad to help him so he could get home sooner. I was cleaning the auditorium when he entered the balcony with a thirty-foot ladder. He placed two legs on the floor of the higher row and two legs on the seats on the lower row. He climbed to the last rung and stretched to reach a burned-out light bulb. I was terrified! A fall would kill him. He was about sixty feet off the ground. I was yelling for him to get down! He said he was fine, and he would be done in a moment. He finished and finally reached the safety of the floor. I was shaking. I am a very positive person, but not that day. Fear overwhelmed me. All I could see was my dad's broken, dead body on the seats of the main floor. When we got home, I told Mom what happened. Dad never changed the light bulbs again.

As much as I tried to keep a low profile, I managed to find other boys who were trying to keep low profiles. I will use fake names to protect their identities. Joe was a heavy boy. I was "stout," and he was larger than me. The second boy was Bob. He looked like any average boy in sixth grade. His only reason for being with Joe and myself was his way of dealing with people. He would speak out of turn, he was loud, and he couldn't follow the topic of discussion. He was an outcast for being a boy! Our little trio lasted until we graduated.

From a child's perspective, reaching senior high seemed to take eight years instead of four years. High school was supposed to be a time of building new relationships, focusing on a career, and developing social and life skills. Since I was now a teenager, I felt I knew everything about life. I knew very little about life. For me, they were years of growth and setbacks.

My setbacks included a broken leg, almost failing wood shop, taking a typing class, and failing German and chemistry. Some of my victories included working for the school newspaper, driving, meeting Diane, and giving my life to Jesus.

I now understand that everything was being used by God to create me into the man he wanted. The hard times taught me to draw closer to him, to trust him more and more. The good times allowed me to experience the peace of resting in him. *God understands what we need, when we need it, and how to present it to us.* The question becomes, do we agree with God on what we need? In other words, who has the authority to define the need, the created or the Creator?

I took a typing class because I loved the English language. I made the choice to learn typing instead of taking a shop class. I thought my choice was a good career move. This was the era when boys learned to do "men's work" while the girls learned "women's work" like cooking, housekeeping, and raising children.

The school years exposed me to life outside of my home and church. I was blessed with teachers who managed to teach me something. From friend to foe, I lived through those years. The most important decision I made was giving my life to Jesus.

How is your life? Are you trying to handle life by yourself? Is there any valid reason to reject Jesus? You allowed people to teach you; why not Jesus? Jesus is the perfect teacher. His classroom is the Holy Bible. When was the last time you entered his classroom?

Father, I need Jesus. I open my heart to Jesus. Thank you for loving me. I ask you to be with me every day. In Jesus's name, Amen.

(August 14, 2023)

The True Me

There is a better *me* somewhere in the world.
The *me* I see in the mirror, none should behold.
I find there are times when I disappoint myself.
When I look inside of me and wonder, what else?

There is an old saying, "I am my own worst enemy."
Perhaps that could be true for me.
I know there is a proper way to live each day,
The searching *me*, this is true, has found the way!

I declare the truth; a truth that is far beyond *me*.
God has given truth a name, the holy name of Jesus.
Jesus said, "Come unto me." I'm sure you
know what happened to *me*.
The loneliness of *me* was completed in the "*us*" of Jesus!

I have learned of the endless love of Jesus.
From birth to resurrection, for all eternity.
Jesus is the *me* I need to be!
Jesus, take my *me*, let it be forever *us*!

There is, indeed, a better *me*, not found in the world.
I found my true self, my real *me*, in Jesus the Lord.
Only in Jesus am I made complete and whole.
The more I submit to Jesus, the more I become truly *me*!

(January 1, 2023)

My Declaration

The task lay before me waiting to be done.
My thoughts were scattered like fallen leaves.
I was a soldier with a battle to be won.
So, I started my part on my knees.

Please guide me Jesus, my Savior and my King.
I claim you as my Lord, God's Only Son.
To you I give praise and of you I sing.
The battle I face you have already won!

The distractions are many.
The enemy rages.
They are hollow and empty.
I serve the Rock of Ages!

In you, Lord, I find Divine Power.
You are the First and the Last.
I seek you every hour.
You gave me a future and forgot my past!

May my trust in you be deeper every day.
May my service be pleasing to you.
I will listen to what you say.
I will do all you want me to do!

Humbly I bow before my true Father.
Here I am use me.
Jesus is like none other.
His glory is all I seek!

(February 8, 2023)

My Thoughts:

Chapter 2

The Children

Moments in Time

Shakespeare wrote, "All the world's a stage." I offer a slight change, "All the world's a series of moments in time." Small children have a very narrow concept of time. Their days seem very long. Most adults, however, try to control their days with schedules. Older adults experience a blending of both concepts. Individual days seem to be long, while the months seem to speed by in a rush.

The following moments in time come from my own life. I was born in 1953, meaning I have gone from the days of the slide rule to the dawning of artificial intelligence. It might even be said that I went from cranking a phone to being the old crank on the phone! My memories are mostly positive. I was blessed with loving parents who loved God. We were not rich by earthly standards. We were rich beyond measure in God's love. God's love is given to us in Jesus Christ. Why should we struggle without him living in our lives? Why would we place upon our children our struggles when Jesus waits for us to find salvation and sanctification in him? Shouldn't we desire the best life possible for our children? Now is the time to ask Jesus to break the old chains, to give us new lives that will heal the entire family. Let us agree with Joshua, "As for me and my house, we will serve the Lord."

When I was a young child, my mom got a used clothes washer. It was a white circular tub with an electrically powered double wooden roller unit attached to the back of the tub. It had wheels and hoses to attach to the sink, making it portable. This meant our laundry was done in the kitchen. Before the clothes were hung outside to dry, they were run through the rollers to remove excess water. It was very easy to get a finger caught in those rollers. I spent lots of time watching Mom do the laundry. She even taught me to use those rollers safely! Does it seem odd that I remember those days? To me, they are fond memories because Mom included me in her busy day.

My dad was always willing to try new things, even if he had no idea of the right way to accomplish the task. When in doubt, improvise! Sometimes he would let me be his helper, which usually meant I was in his way or I was slowing down the completion of the work. It didn't matter, we were spending time together. For several years, he would go into the basement of the apartment building to shovel coal into the furnace. This deal with the landlord gave us a lower rent.

When I was ten, Dad allowed me to work at the local hardware store. I was allowed to work after school and on Saturday. I swept the floors, dusted items as needed, and stocked the shelves. One day the owner took me to his lodge to deliver boxes of alcohol. I was raised in an alcohol-free home. We did not drink any form of alcohol. I was very bothered by supplying alcohol to the lodge. I told my parents what I had done, and they told me I was not to blame. They still loved me and so did God. Dad called the store owner and told him that I would no longer work for him and that he had been wrong to make a young boy deliver alcohol to his lodge.

My parents had unexpected ways to bring joy and laughter into my life. One day Mom, Dad, my friend, and I took a ride on a country road. My friend and I had no idea what my parents were about to do for us. Suddenly, Mom made the car speed up a small incline. The car crested the top, and we found ourselves floating in the air. We were weightless! Four times we rose from our seats! What an experience! We were laughing and laughing! Was it dangerous? Yes. Was it thrilling fun? Absolutely!

These are just some examples of the impact actions can have on children. *Simple things simply shape how a person deals with life.* It is just as important to show others they are special in our lives as it is to tell them. God established the family format of dad, mom, and children to give the children a blessed home, leading to an ever more loving relationship with others and Jesus.

It doesn't take a lot of money to shape a child's life. It takes imagination and, sometimes, the willingness to act just a little bit like a child.

Think about God. He created us, only to see the bond between us broken by sin. So he sent Jesus to restore our relationship. Jesus became like us, except without sin. He was raised by a mom and dad who loved him and God. He was their son too.

His first miracle was done to please his mother. He was showing us that his love for Mary was reflecting her love for him.

There is one more important reason to raise children in the love of Jesus: the salvation of their souls.

(July 8, 2023)

The Ocean

It's the ocean above me, it's the ocean around me.
Am I drowning in this sea, or is it God with me?
I'm in the ocean of God's love, fear not, I am not drowning.
It is the love of Jesus for me that is overwhelming!

I see God's Glory all around me, the Glory of eternity,
The Glory of God's Majesty, Jesus is God's Glory!
Jesus is above me; Jesus is around me,
I am living in the ocean of Jesus's Love!

I gave my life to Jesus, who took my sins at Calvary.
Now I'm living for my Savior, in the ocean of his Love.
It's the ocean above me, it's the ocean around me,
I am living in the ocean, the ocean of God's Love!

(November 2, 2022)

Three Times Blessed

The following events really happened to me. The first one happened when I was a very young child. I remember just a little bit of the event. My parents told me much of the story when I was older. My parents did not embellish the story. What I am going to share is true. All three are true. I am three times blessed because the Lord spared my life three times.

The first event happened when I was a young boy. I was riding in the back seat of a four-door car. There were no seatbelts and no child car seats. The car door lock could be opened by pulling upward on a metal knob. The door was easily opened by pulling on a lever-type handle. The front doors opened like car doors today. The rear door opened by swinging toward the back of the car. Both doors were locked at the central pillar located at the center of the car.

I remember opening the back door. The rest comes from my parents. I immediately fell out of the car, hitting the top of my head on the curb where the top and side meet, forming a seven shape. My skull split open, exposing my brain. My mom was able to rush me to the local hospital. (There were no cell phones and no 911 services.) Dad was at work in Williamsport, a town twelve miles away. Due to medical issues, he was not allowed to drive.

While the hospital tended to me, Dad had flagged down a Greyhound bus to get back home. The bus driver went off his route to take my dad directly to the hospital! While my dad was going in the front door, I was being loaded into an ambulance at the back of the hospital. He made it just in time to get into the ambulance that was going right back to Williamsport! Mom had to drive the car so they could get home.

Because of my critical injury, arrangements had been made for a two motorcycle police escort to the hospital. We went full speed through the city. In fact, the motorcycles were so hot they were smoking!

This accident happened back in the late 1950s era. My parents were told not to get their hopes up. No one expected me to survive. They truly underestimated my parents' faith! My parents loved Jesus completely. They spread the news that I needed prayer, and the people responded. Heaven was bombarded with prayers for my healing. God agreed. I don't know if my healing was immediate or extended. God healed me, and that is all that mattered. Mom told me they had been warned by the doctors that I might end up with brain damage. Our gracious God granted me a complete healing!

How intensely do we pray? How much faith do we present to God? During our daily devotions, do we have the same approach to God as in times of an emergency? When does *faith* become more than just another word?

*****

It was April 30, 2010, and I was sitting in my car at a red light on US-31. It was close to 2:30 a.m., and I was on my way to work. While waiting for the light to change color, I glanced at the rear-view mirror and saw two gigantic headlights. As I lifted my foot off the break, the fully loaded trailer truck hit me while going 60 mph. My Malibu was flung off the road like a child's toy. When it finally stopped spinning, the back seat had been shoved under the driver's seat. I was sitting on both seats! I was able to find my glasses without turning my head.

Suddenly, the back door opened, and a man crawled into the car. He was an off duty paramedic! He grabbed my head and told me to keep my head straight while the other paramedic checked on the truck driver. The other driver had fallen asleep. I felt much better knowing that he was all right.

The ambulance arrived, and those paramedics took me to the local hospital. A few hours later, I was taken in another ambulance to a trauma hospital in Indianapolis. The cot gave me a view out of the back window. I told the paramedic who rode with me that the last thing I wanted to see was a trailer truck. Of course, almost the entire trip we were followed by a trailer truck! That brought all of us a good laugh!

I was allowed to go home later that day wearing a collar, lots of medicine, and strict instructions to do nothing. I also had an appointment to see one of the best specialists for broken necks. The doctor told me that he had never seen a neck broken like my neck! He said I should have been dead. Then he said I should have been paralyzed. His last warning has stayed with me the most: someday, I could turn my head just the wrong way and be paralyzed.

Here is where my faith grows in the amazing power of God. That accident happened almost thirteen years ago. Here is the incredible part: not only was I healed, but I have also never had any type of headache since the accident!

That was a very trying time for everyone who loved me. Many friends stepped up to help us. Isn't that how God intended for us to behave? Jesus calls us into his family when we give him our lives. Family. The family of God. Our eternal family.

Is our heavenly family part of our daily lives or just a Sunday family? Do we value God's family as much as we value our earthly family? Do we truly understand the importance of doing things for each other? Do we value the times we get to spend together?

*****

The third event started in January 2012 but wasn't recognized until June fourth of 2012. That was the date that confirmed I had liver cancer. It had been growing for quite a while and was stage three. What I am about to reveal was possible only through the love God had for me. He has blessed me even when I don't deserve his blessings. When I learned about the extent of cancer, my first thought was, *I am going to live.* I claimed victory and thanked the Lord that I was allowed to have the cancer instead of someone else.

My parents were an important influence on my faith and optimism. Their own physical challenges were handled by their faith in God. They taught me to believe the same way. The day before my surgery, a chaplain from work paid me a visit. Before leaving, he told me that I had made him feel better!

Allow me to reverse time to the events after the initial diagnosis. The next two months were filled with blood samples, tests, and visits to doctors. My surgeon was a Christian. We immediately made a connection in Christ. During one of my visits, he told me he had contacted some specialists, who had advised him that our proposed surgery was ill-advised. I would not survive the surgery, so I should just enjoy the time.

The doctor agreed with me to have the surgery. It lasted ten hours with two thirds of my liver being removed. The liver is the only organ that regenerates. I have a fully functioning liver, and I have been cancer free since 2012.

There is so much more to this story, but this was the brief version.

How should believers respond to major critical events? What role does our faith in God play? How do we balance the response of the flesh and the response of the soul?

Should we respond like Job or his three friends? Do we tend to minimize or exaggerate? Do we take on the role of the loner, or do we seek out others' advice?

Do we turn to Jesus, or do we turn *away*? Is our cry, "*Why me?*" or "*Here I am*"?

These three times happened in my life. It is my prayer that you will spend time in prayer, seeking God's guidance in your life. The best preparation for any emergency is found in God. We are encouraged to have emergency plans for our homes and cars. Do we have plans approved by God for emergencies that affect our souls?

My friends, every answer for every problem is found in our ever-loving Lord.

Thank you, Father God, for your love. Amen.

(February 23, 2023)

Realistic

Some people wonder about me, I'm just too optimistic,
With Jesus living in my heart, I say I'm realistic.
Let me make a little list, like Paul did in the Bible,
To show the Power of Christ, he is more than capable!

There was the day my skull was cracked; would I live or die?
Much later it was cancer, but God kept me alive.
Then a trailer truck hit my car. With God did I thrive.
By the Power of my Risen Lord, God has kept me alive!

Look at your own life, what is it that you see?
Do you see God's Power? Do you see God's Love?
If you choose to love Jesus, if you give him your sin,
He will redeem you, please, invite Jesus in!

With God my Father, Jesus my Savior, the Holy Spirit, too.
A smile forms on my face, what else should I do?
I'm in love with my Risen Savior, Jesus is my Lord.
God is my Father; he has given me my life.
The Holy Spirit guides me in God's Word.
Some day the Glory of Heaven is where I will abide.

Am I too optimistic? No, I am realistic.
All that happens is really a blessing, an opportunity.
For me to share the Power of God, his Love and Victory.

Jesus gives me true reality; Jesus gives me his Victory!
So, optimistic I will be, since Jesus is my Reality!

(November 17, 2022)

Becoming Moses

Pennsylvania is the home of a forty-seven-mile-long gorge known as the Pennsylvania Grand Canyon. This is a heavily forested area with a river and some hiking trails. Today it is part of a trail system for all kinds of recreation. What is true today doesn't apply to the 1960s era.

Back in the era of the hippies, flower power, and social unrest, my family found community and fellowship in our local church. Every time the doors were open, we were there—my grandparents, my parents, and me. The five of us had our own pew. Literally. The little brass plate on the end of it made it official.

Grandpa sat on the end at the center aisle. Grandma was next, then me, followed by Mom and Dad. Grandpa would always seem to be sleeping until he would say "Amen" in a voice loud enough to wake up my dad, who managed to sleep with Mom poking him in the ribs with her elbow. The pastor understood that Grandpa was old and did his best to stay awake. He also knew that my dad's medicine made him sleep. He really tried to stay awake, but the medicine was too strong.

What was so amazing about our little church was the love and respect they shared with each other. No one judged my family as incapable of doing things for the Lord. My dad served as a greeter and usher. My mom kept the Sunday school records and sang in the choir. My grandpa had a marvelous bass singing voice that added a richness to the hymns. My grandma was known for her ability to make quilts and was in high demand with the Women's Missionary Society.

Me? I was deeply involved with the youth group. I was either the mascot or the leader, it depended on the day. For example, there was the day our youth group went to the Pennsylvania Grand Canyon. That was the day I earned the nickname of Moses.

I have always been an outgoing person, after the initially polite status required when meeting people for the first time. At the time of our youth group trip, I was the duly elected leader of the group. Unknown to everyone, I would sometimes get lost in a new area since, being a male, I never asked for directions.

After our group had looked through the pay-to-view binoculars, we decided to go on a hike into the valley. The adults told us to be careful, avoid strangers, don't get hurt, and to be back in two hours. I don't think they realized we were all teenagers. What fun would it be if all we did was march single file for an hour, turn around, and march back?

After we were out of range for them to hear us, we started acting like teenagers. We promptly forgot about their warnings and simply acted like kids. It was fun! After an unknown amount of time had passed, we started wondering if we were lost. I reassured them we were not lost. We just needed to go "that" way, and we would be back in no time.

They should have ignored me and gone in the opposite direction. It was almost an hour later when we realized we were truly lost. There were no cell phones. No watches with tracking capabilities. We had a paper map, which was useless in the woods. That was when we saw the hunter. He was a big man with a long beard. He wore hunting clothes and carried a huge rifle. He looked really scary. Thank goodness we mustered up our courage and told him we were lost. At first, he acted gruffly and said, "Thought so."

We realized we were talking to a stranger with a rifle. Would any of us make it back alive? The man seemed really mean. Finally, he let out a laugh and reassured us he wasn't a mass murderer and gave us directions back to the adults. We arrived back just before dark. The adults were not pleased. It took several months of me being called Moses until I was able to forget the great misadventure.

What about the real Moses? A child of slavery who was raised as a prince of Egypt. A murderer who fled Egypt to meet God forty years later as a shepherd. A reluctant leader with a speech problem who led the entire nation of Israel on a forty-year trek in the wilderness. A man who loved and obeyed God so well that he was known as the humblest human. Perhaps we should look at this man who met with Jesus at his Transfiguration.

Let's look beyond the obvious to discover the deeper truth revealed in the life of Moses. What we learn will be wasted unless we apply it to our own lives. What does Jesus want for us? Doesn't he want us to study his Word and make it a part of our lives?

Moses saw the burning bush and decided he was going to find out what was happening on the mountain. He had curiosity and courage. Curiosity and courage can lead us into the woods to get lost, or they can take us to the throne of God. Life is more adventurous when we let the Lord know that we are willing to answer his calling.

Moses had no idea where he was going. He was the human leader, but he was also the first follower. The Bible clearly tells us that God used the pillar of fire by night and cloud by day to lead the people. Moses followed the fire. The people followed him. *The best leader is the best follower.* A poor leader is a poor follower. We need to be people who follow Christ. Jesus is our Leader. The more we become followers, the better lives we will live. Jesus taught about the first being last. A humble leader's authority is not his own, it belongs to God. Jesus also said that he only spoke what God told him to speak. Jesus always humbles himself to God. Shouldn't we?

Moses failed to properly obey God and was not allowed to enter the promised land. Was this too harsh? No, not at all. Moses had developed an incredibly close relationship with God. This relationship was so deep that Moses appeared at the Transfiguration! How much better would our lives be if we truly kept God first in our lives?

Moses had to learn to say no. Hundreds of people would surround him every day so he could be the judge. He learned that it was necessary to have other men assume the roles of judges. He couldn't keep up with the demands. Yes, there are times when we need to say no. God values family life and wants our personal lives to be based on his Word. We would do well to study the life of Moses.

Perhaps being called Moses was a compliment after all.

What to Do

Children are so innocent, willing to learn.
They learn to share, be polite, and take their turns.
With something new they might get confused,
They stop and say, "I don't know what to do!"

When adults face something new,
They may say, "I don't know what to do!"
Today we learn at many schools,
Be it quantum mechanics or the golden rule!

Moses stood before the sea while Pharaoh drew near.
The people were trapped, they cried out in fear!
Moses stood there. What to do, what to do?
God said, "Don't just stand there, here is what you do."

If we love the Lord, we should love to serve.
It may be scary, but God calms our nerves.
Is there something that challenges you?
Then you have discovered what you can do!

We worship the only God who can do!
Jesus died and rose again for me and you!
He removes our sins with his Love so true!
Our Lord helps us say, "I know what to do!"

(July 1, 2023)

Childhood Fear and Terror

Most of my childhood was spent in a small apartment in Jersey Shore, Pennsylvania. My bedroom was eight feet by ten feet. The only window was a square skylight that opened onto the hallway. This allowed slightly cooler air in my room along with the neighbor's noise and cooking odors. I would lie in bed and stare at that window, and stare, and stare. Until that night, I had a terrible nightmare. Over fifty years later, I still remember that dream. Now I see it as an event that was the result of staring at that window.

There was another event in my young life that frightened me. At the time, and at my age, the fear was very real and very intimidating. I was spending the night with my cousins. My aunt and uncle were away on some errand. The oldest cousin would not be back for a while. That left my two cousins, Tim and Larry.

Since we were alone, we did things that little boys do. We watched a scary movie on the television, ate popcorn, and started teasing each other. All of this led to telling ghost stories. One of my cousins appeared with their vacuum cleaner. It was old and noisy with a large headlight. The more he chased me with the vacuum cleaner, the more fear welled up inside of me. Within a few moments, I was totally frightened. Fear overwhelmed me. I saw a door in the kitchen. I just had to reach that door so I could get away from my fear. I could escape! Just as I opened the door, my cousin lunged at me with the vacuum. I stepped backward without looking. I had to get away!

I stepped backward into nothing. The door led down to the garage. I fell down the stairs. Almost twenty feet. About a minute later, the garage door opened as my aunt and uncle got home. They got me back upstairs, and my cousins were punished. I was shaken up, but not hurt. The Lord had protected me! How easily I was frightened of a vacuum cleaner!

Children are easily frightened. They are truly innocent when they are babies. As they mature, they are exposed to more and more to the world. They usually must make sense of everything they see and hear by themselves. Children need parents to be responsible for them.

Jesus said to his disciples, "Let the little children come to me, and do not hinder them, for the kingdom of Heaven belongs to such as these" (Matthew 19:14).

Paul wrote, "Children, obey your parents in the Lord, for this is right" (Ephesians 6:1).

Fear is one of Satan's greatest tools. Children need to be protected from fear. What can parents, and the church, do to help the children? The following suggestions should be adapted for the various stages of growth:

1. Focus on Christ. Keeping Jesus first in our lives with family prayers, Bible readings, and worship.
2. Actively monitor what your children are learning at school.
3. Monitor what they see on television and the Internet.
4. Talk with them! Ask them what they are thinking. Help them deal with their fears.
5. Hug them. Tell them you love them. Treat them like Jesus treated the children.
6. Remember, they are children. Let them be children!

Children are a blessing from God. May God's love flow freely in our families.

(April 13, 2023)

Some Thoughts about Childhood

Was my childhood different from other children? Generally speaking, no. When asking about specific details, the answer is yes. That is true about most children. Let's explore some of my personal history for some answers to our question.

When I was a small child, I could go to my parents if something upset me. The same was true for my grandparents. The unexpected fall that made me bleed. The toy that broke. (Did I do that?) Let us not forget the times when I felt ignored or I didn't get my way. I did not realize how taxing that was for my parents. Children do not think about the stresses they place on their parents. Things were beginning to change in my life. My body was growing faster than my emotions. I was comfortable being a child, especially an only child. I was loved and safe. I had all the attention. Should it matter if I was getting older? Didn't I deserve the special treatment?

Children want and need consistency. They are, in the truest sense, young souls trying to learn about life in our world. The world confuses us. Imagine how children get confused! Where am I going with this concept? One day my parents told me a few words that changed my world: "You are a big boy now."

I was immediately thrust out of my comfort zone. I did not want to be a big boy! I wanted things to stay the same! Did I understand my feelings or what I was experiencing? No, I was a child. Only by looking back do I understand my childhood in a new way. Back then, I had to live through the changes.

That was when the nightmares began. Why do children have such dreams? I propose their loss of security is the major factor in nightmares. If the children have unresolved emotional stresses, they will deal with nightmares, until they can replace them with a renewed sense of security.

Are we pushing our children into adulthood? Are we allowing them to be influenced by others? Should we limit their exposure to stressors? Do we understand the difference between protection and smothering? I knew a boy whose mother protected him from everything. He was under her total control. It was so very sad. He was placed in a class for children with special needs for learning.

She passed away a few years later. Only then did his dad remove her rules and told him he could make his own decisions. My friend was finally allowed to be himself. He immediately revealed that he was a very intelligent student. In due time, he was married, had a family, and was a respected member of his town.

As I grew older, the nightmares began to fade. Doesn't it seem that one thing replaces another in our lives? Have you ever said, "I just wish I could get a break"? I was now in junior high school, perhaps the most awkward age to live. I had adjusted to being a "big boy" by growing older. We all know that stage of life. The body continues to grow faster than maturity. Children grow "faster than weeds." The voice begins to change. The world seems to turn against them. Most children want to be adults without giving up their childhood.

Each child will respond differently to the stresses they experience. Back then, I had no idea how to handle my stressors. I was at the age of withdrawal. Since I was a "big boy," I reasoned my parents would prefer my keeping my thoughts and emotions to myself. Internalizing is the worst possible thing for children to attempt. I was one of the fat kids in school. I was ignored, teased, and bullied. I never fought back. I would get home and spend my time in my room. I never told my parents.

Parents, grandparents, and other adults in the family, how aware are you of your child's emotional life? Do you know the child's daily experiences? Are you aware of how they deal with the cruelty of other children? Have you ever thought that every day is a new day for children? A new day to be marginalized, teased, mocked, and bullied? Are your children reclusive? Do they turn to you for help?

High school was much worse. I was a nontypical teenager because of my Christian beliefs. I was fat, opinionated, and lacking in the art of tactfulness. It is no wonder that I was teased, mocked, and often threatened. I had two friends who were also living outside of the school's general population. I had one other classmate who was my friend outside of school but not in school.

This discrimination was somewhat balanced by the church youth group. The children in the youth group came from different grades and different schools. I felt more accepted by them.

One day at school, a boy approached me to invite me to his house that afternoon. I accepted, so we rode our bicycles toward his house. We turned into an alley, and he suddenly attacked me! I did not fight back. I just tried to protect my face. He hit me a few times and stopped. I asked him why he attacked me. He confessed to being pressured by his "friends" to beat me up. I told him I would not fight him. I told him I would still forgive him, even if he kept hitting me. That was when he gave me the look of surprise. He said he was sorry and could we still be friends? Yes! We had a great time together at his house, and I went home having a new friend.

Life continued. Does that sound rather dull? Does it sound scary or threatening? For a child, it has the potential for all three. In the same day. The world is very complicated. Adults, how are you doing with teaching your children about God? Adam and Eve sinned. Life continued. There was Noah's flood. Life continued. Jesus died at Calvary. Life continued. Then Jesus rose from the grave, and everything changed. Death was defeated, and life continued, not just physically but spiritually! We must teach our children that God loves them and he is alive and will give them peace and comfort.

I was drawing closer to being a man. I was starting to think like an adult. My parents were very shocked when I returned from a youth camp and told them I had met the girl I was going to marry! They both laughed at me! That was all right with me. She accepted my proposal on our second date. We were married almost forty-three years before she went to live with Jesus in heaven. Life continued.

Life continued, and I am no longer a "big boy." I am now a senior citizen. Our thinking changes; our physical abilities change. Here is some good news: God never changes! His love for us is eternal, from birth to death. God is always God. I still have my emotions, and I still have God. Praise his holy name!

Do you struggle with your emotions? Are you aware that your emotional life directly affects your children's lives? *The more you surrender your emotions to God, the more they will come into agreement with God's emotions.* Yes, God has emotions. We do not need to suffer or struggle with our emotions. Jesus is the Savior of our soul, heart, mind, body, and our emotions. Does this seem too simplistic? Shouldn't it be harder? No!

Jesus Christ is alive! He sacrificed himself for every part of our lives. He wants to give us victory over our emotions. Jesus shed his blood to buy our emotional salvation. It is simple. We ask Jesus to be the Lord of our emotional life. Then we go and live every day as Jesus leads us.

Our life journeys may be different, but God is still God. We have Jesus as our Lord and Savior. We have the Holy Spirit who guides us daily. Our lives must be focused on Jesus. Children watch the adults. Do they see us in love with God and Jesus? Do they see us practicing what we preach?

Remember the children. If we fail to raise them into a Christian adulthood, the sinful world will raise them to reject God, leading them into a life of misery and sin. The burden falls upon the adults. Children are not mature enough to understand everything that happens to and around them. The adults have one very important duty: bring the children to Jesus. Be there with them. Do they see Jesus in us?

(December 3, 2023)

I Am a Child

I am a child. My home is dark, but warm. I can feel my heart beating. I hear things. I don't know what the sounds mean. They just make me feel loved. I feel safe here. I'm glad I am here.

I am a child. Now I know who talked to me. Mom is always with me. She holds me and feeds me. She is soft and warm. Dad makes me laugh. He makes funny faces and silly sounds. He is big and strong, yet when he holds me, I feel secure and protected. I feel safe in his arms.

I am a child. I can walk! Just like my mom and dad and my sister! I love my family. They give me food, clothes, a home, and lots of toys! I love to play! Sometimes I get hungry, upset, or hurt; so I cry. I don't know the words. Words are hard.

I am a child. I am older now. Elementary school is boring, hard, dangerous, funny, and necessary. I don't like homework. Home is my favorite place. My sister and I love to play games. Mom and Dad must work. I like the babysitter.

I am a child. Junior high school is a whole new world. A world I never knew existed. Mom and Dad have no idea what I deal with every day. They don't ask, and I don't tell. I can't tell them. That is the way things work in school.

"I am a child!"

The officer ignored me. "You have the right…"

I decided to ignore him. Stupid cop. What did he know anyway? Did he know I was really eighteen? Wait! What's this? I'm getting a mug shot? And they called my parents! I had no idea I would get arrested! What have I done?

"I am a child" didn't stop the police. I was found guilty and was given community service with a requirement to attend counseling. The time I spent in jail really shook me up. Someone told me about a group meeting at a church. I didn't know why, but that invitation would not leave me alone. I had to go, just once, to get the idea out of my head.

"I am a child of God." The man leading the group spoke with absolute assurance. I had never heard such confidence. His words captivated me. He spoke about his life in Jesus. I knew I would be back.

"I am a child" had been my protection and my limitation. I had hidden my entire life behind those words. I tried desperately to justify my decisions by wrapping them in an illusion of childhood innocence.

"I am a child of God," he repeated. Listen to how 1 John 3:1 reads: "See what great love the Father has given us that we should be called God's children—and we are!" (CSB).

I am a child of God! That thought was like a warm blanket on a cold morning. It finally made sense. Me! I am! I looked at the teacher with tears streaming down my face. Compassion leapt from his eyes and touched my very soul. He led me in a prayer of repentance. I felt my sins being washed away! I was a different person! I looked at him with Jesus's love in my heart. There was so much joy in my life I shouted in my loudest voice, "I *AM* a child of God!"

When we allow our children to have more independence, should we still encourage them to share how they felt about their day?

Should parents verify a child's location when they are out with friends?

How many restrictions should be placed on a child? How should they be adjusted for age and maturity?

How should we speak to our children about behaviors that are detrimental to them?

When should children be introduced to Jesus?

Should parents be concerned about the examples they set?

In your opinion, how would you rank the importance of Jesus in your family?

(October 24, 2023)

The Awakening

Something was changing in my life.
What was happening? I could not tell.
Slowly my reality faded. Away it fell.
Sleep gave way to a new day as I opened an eye.

Another day before me, a challenging reality.
The clock warned me, time was moving on.
Thoughts of activities nagged to be done.
Gently the Lord reminded me, *I am all you need.*

Stay here with me, feel my peace upon your soul.
I created you and time, you are mine.
You have given me your heart, give me your mind.
Rest a few moments while I make you whole.

So, I stayed with my mind aware of my Savior.
I gave to him each thought upon my mind.
Random thoughts arose; given to God, no longer mine.
Sweet peace was upon me, I was in God's favor.

Worry, stress, daily pressures wanted me.
Worldly confusion gave no time for God's Holy Word.
I've learned to start each day with Jesus, my Lord.
Every day lived with Jesus is another day of Divine Victory!

(June 30, 2023)

My Thoughts:

Chapter 3

The Valley

Down in the Dump

This story begins in 1921 when my dad was born. My mom was born in 1926. My dad was eight, and my mom was three when the Great Depression started in 1929. This was the worst depression in American history. Most of the banks closed. The stock market not only crashed, but it also crumbled. There was no FDIC to ensure the money deposited by the public, so people lost everything.

My mom's parents were better off because my grandpa had a very good position and had saved his money. My dad's parents were less fortunate. They always struggled financially. The depression hurt everyone. My mom's family experienced financial trouble while my dad's family really struggled. The depression officially ended on December 7, 1941, when Japan attacked Pearl Harbor.

From eight years old to twenty years old, Dad spent twelve years growing up in poverty. Mom was three in 1929 and fifteen when the depression ended. She spent twelve years growing up frugally. After everything they experienced as children, they had to live through World War Two! There were all kinds of things being rationed because the factories had been forced to make items for the war. It ended December 2, 1945. My parents spent the time of twenty-four years being emotionally and socially trained to accept poverty as their lifestyle. For example, when Dad was a child, the family would go and harvest tomatoes because the farmer would let them eat the tomatoes!

Let's jump into the 1960s era. I was seven in 1960. My parents were always poor. My dad always found work, usually as a janitor. The highest pay he ever received was $42 a week. He made a deal with the landlord to keep the coal furnace full of coal for a discount on the rent. My mom and I would go to the local firehouse for free food from the government.

Now we come to the town dump. The town had property where all trash was dumped over a hill. Paper items were put into dumpsters that would be emptied into a furnace for burning to make electricity.

There were no fences. People were allowed to drive around the property to reach the bottom of the hill. Why? To scavenge!

Our small town had the "rich" people and the "poor" people. No one was rich; it just seemed that way to most of the population. So we would take the old Chevy station wagon, go to the bottom of the hill, and look for things we could use. Yes, we had to watch for items being tossed down the hill!

We usually found useful items too!

Going to the dump was an adventure for a young boy. Those were days of innocence. We never thought about germs. Safety was having our eyes open for more junk rolling down the hill. Those days are long gone.

What does this have to do with the Lord? Many people have had circumstances in their lives that have discouraged them. The sources of such treatment are as different as they are common. That is, no matter the delivery system, the result is the same. Satan will us all types of things to make someone feel like unwanted trash tossed over a hill.

But there is a flaw in Satan's plan. He works hard to get people depressed, only to have Jesus come along, see us as precious, and rescue us from the dump! Jesus sees our true value! That is Satan's weakness! He cannot see value in anyone! Please consider this question: who determines our value? Is it God who created us, or he who seeks to destroy? Is it God who sees our value, or he who doesn't see our value?

Jesus said, "I have come that they may have life, and have it to the full" (John 10:10).

John said, "He who has the Son has life" (1 John 5:12).

Paul wrote, "Therefore, if anyone is in Christ, he is a new creation, the old has gone, the new has come!" (2 Corinthians 5:17).

Father, thank you for showing me my true value. I am worth your blood at Calvary. I am worth the empty tomb. I claim Jesus as my Lord and Savior! Amen!

Now go down to the dump. Take Jesus with you. Find another precious soul and help rescue them. Show them just how much God loves them!

(April 8, 2023)

A Reflective Moment

The mirror was secured upon the wall,
With decorative fixtures held by screws.
It was not wide, but it was long,
So, I could see down to my shoes.

Most would see a simple mirror.
Not convex, nor concave, no funny shapes to see.
It would show a reflection, far or near,
But I saw more than just me.

Perhaps I should share what I could see.
A cautionary vision I should tell.
Do you really think I only saw me?
Prepare yourself! Will I see Heaven or Hell?

The thing I saw amazed my eyes.
The surface looked like me in every way.
But what I saw seemed dead, not alive.
The more I watched, the more it faded away.

Then I could see a most horrible sight,
Darkness that absorbed every soul.
An endless void of hopeless night.
Full of sin and pain; no love, no hope

That image. It frightened me!
I could feel it taking control!
There had to be more to see!
Something, or someone, to save my soul!

That must have been the thought I needed.
It was my desperate prayer of hope.
Someway, somehow, my prayer was heeded.
Jesus was there to claim my soul!

As I started to focus on my Lord,
The image changed in part.
The void of sin was filled with God's Word.
As the mirror changed, so did my heart.

The Light of Christ was shining through.
What started in my heart changed the mirror.
The Love of God was changing me, too!
Jesus was filling me! He was so near!

With all my heart I cried out,
Jesus, forgive me, save me, be my Lord!
He cleansed me completely, without a doubt.
Now the mirror shows me Jesus, my Living Lord!

(September 17, 2023)

Why?

Why?

The room was dark. The windows were closed. The curtains were drawn. The lights were off. A towel sealed the gap below the door. The only light came from the lightning storm raging at the house, beating against it, trying to destroy it with electrified bolts of death. Booming thunder followed the stabbing lightning, echoing the rage. The deafening pounding of the rain beating on the house seemed determined to break a window. The noise added to my misery. The turmoil inside of me equaled that of the external storm. A personal storm that no one seemed to understand. A storm that always returned to just one word.

Why?

There was a sudden chill in the air. I shook like the leaves on the tree as they were beating on the window. I curled up on the chair and covered myself with a throw. I just wanted to hide from everything and everyone. The storm outside of me echoed the storm raging inside of me. My thoughts raced like lightning, striking with powerful energy throughout my mind. My headache throbbed with every cracking thunder. Hiding under the throw did not bring comfort. Just the opposite. I felt more loneliness and pain.

Why? Why, oh, why?

Somehow, the darkness seemed to be deepening. Although I could not see it getting darker, I could sense it. A black hole that was growing larger and darker. I could feel it. It seemed to have substance. I tried to move, but the darkness felt like a straitjacket. I was frozen inside total, absolute darkness. I felt lost inside the void. I was alone. All alone. The room, the storm—everything was gone. The blackness was absolute. It had crept into my thoughts. It had claimed me. I was alone and afraid. So very afraid. I knew it would keep burrowing into my body and soul. I would be lost forever in this horrible, dreadful void. I had only one thought: *Why? Why me?*

A voice seemed to come from the void. A cruel, vindictive, hateful, judgmental voice that I could not ignore. It was laced with terror and fear. Every word felt like bile in my throat, except it was in my mind. That voice made me feel rotted and corrupted in my soul. That voice considered me as a personal toy. Unspeakable horrors would be my eternal existence. Its desire for my soul was unquenchable.

Why?

Was this the end of me? Was I going to die? In the depth of that darkness came a realization: I had done this to myself! I was the one who had lived by his own rules. I remembered every lie, every action, every word, every time I chose my own interests over those of others, every failure and shamefulness. The voice mocked me over and over.

In sheer desperation, I screamed aloud, "God, help me!"

The response was immediate and left me unprepared.

Why?

What! Why are you asking me why? All right, God, I'll tell you why! I don't want to go to hell! Look at me! I am scared to death! I'm caught in this evil void. I can't move. I can't see. I'm caught in an evil trap! Where am I? Am I dead? I don't even know why I thought of you! Are you going to do something? Help me!

There was only silence. The silence began to grow. It was the smallest of thoughts, then it started to move into my arms. It moved slowly, steadily through my chest and right leg. I could feel it. Then it moved into my left leg. It moved slower and slower. I felt it stop. It was at that moment I realized God was answering my prayer. The thought burst into my mind the way a firework bursts in the sky. It was a new thought, a holy revelation enlightening my life. What I thought was silence was the love of Jesus Christ, expressed through the Holy Spirit, working to free me from the prison of my own sin!

Why was I like this? Had someone forced me into sin? No, I had chosen sin. The depth of my sin was reached by my own decisions. The void that threatened me was of my own doing. My own sin led me into more sin. Sin was multiplied upon sin.

Why, oh, why, had I thought only of myself? Why? Why had it taken so long for me to realize what I had done? Why had the Lord stopped in my left leg?

Immediately, I was aware of my true reality. God's Son could not be stopped. He had paused. He was waiting for me to become aware of what he was doing. I could feel the evil fighting back, unwilling to release its grip on me. I knew I had to make the most important decision of my life.

"God, I am sorry for my sins. Please forgive me. Please finish what you have started. Please free me from evil!"

I felt the power of Jesus Christ's blood overwhelming the rest of my body. His Holy Spirit was preparing the way for my freedom. This was more than a "feel good" salvation. This was the Blood of the Lamb removing every sin, every failure, everything that had led me to this moment. This was the moment that God moved, and the evil was gone! The darkness was expelled from me! The void was gone! I could move! I tossed off the throw and inhaled a deep breath of God's pure air. That breath matched the Holy Spirit moving into my soul. The storm outside was gone, along with my headache. I opened the drapes to feel the warmth of the sunshine, just as Jesus's forgiveness filled my heart with his love! My salvation was real and complete. I was a child of God!

Why?

That word returned to my thoughts. It still challenged me, but without accusation. Why had I tried running my own life? Did I bother to think how foolish it was to try doing what God does?

I started to recall my life. I was raised to be independent. Society encouraged me to be my own person. Many religions taught that God helps those who help themselves. Others taught that God made us a little lower than the angels so we could handle things since he was busy.

Why?

Why had I believed such things? Why did it take so long for me to realize how much Jesus loved me? Today, I live in the love light of Jesus Christ. Do you? Please ask Jesus to forgive you and love you. Freedom is waiting for you.

A Selfish Death

There once was a man who was quite proud.
He was very wealthy and respected all around.
Land ownership was the game for him.
His land made money for him, again and again.
Hired hands did the work, as he spent time at rest.
"What a great life!" he thought. "I am the best!"

There was a poor fellow who worked for that man.
He kept the animals, saved some money, and had a plan.
He would work faithfully for his wealthy boss,
His boss would make money, he would not suffer loss.
The poor man was often hungry, and often alone.
No family, no wife, a barn was his home.

The harvest was beyond what the rich man expected.
He would use every possible space to keep the crop protected.
With no thought of the poor worker's plight,
He ordered, "Fill everything to the top! Pack it tight!"
He thought, "My business is great! My barns are full!"
So proud and smug, until he heard God say, "You fool!"

"This very night your soul is required of you!"
But my harvest has made the barns full!
I need more time to have a grand harvest party!
We can eat, drink, and celebrate heartily!
I can see it now! Everyone will honor and love me!
I am the greatest farmer! Just wait and see!

"You were, indeed, a rich farmer in this land,
But your crops were made by my command!
I gave you everything to show you, my power.

I SEE JESUS

But you rejected me, until this very hour.
You are a wretched man. Poor and despised.
Hear my words of truth. No more excuses or lies."

The rich man knew he could not say a word.
God's spoken judgment had been heard.
He saw the land and the barns packed tight.
Then he saw the poor worker with a new insight.
His face and clothing shone like the white-hot sun!
His was a glory that rejoiced in what God had done!

As the rich man watched with a new view,
He saw his old body tossed in a tomb.
Then he heard God's enemy say, "Here we are."
"You will spend eternity with me. You will never depart!"
He replied, "What am I doing here? Why me?"
Satan replied, "Why? You rejected God! *You are just like me!*"

How are we living today? What does God see?
Are we selfish, thinking only of "me"?
Will we hear God say, "Welcome home?"
Will we accept God's love or die alone?
Jesus is ready to forgive every sin!
Confess all to Jesus! Open your heart to him!

(July 12, 2023)

Judgment Day

Do you believe a judgment will come?
When we will face God for what was done?
When do our words reveal what we had to say?
Are we ready for the final judgment day?
Just a minute, that isn't fair! We need some way to be prepared.
How can we be accepted when we don't know what is expected?

Jesus spoke about judgment day, because he wants us to be saved.
God wants us to live with him for eternity.
How we live now shapes our destiny.
He said, hunger, thirst, a stranger, almost naked;
sick and a prisoner; a sad, sad state.
There is more than a need for the physical. Our need is spiritual!

Good deeds are done by sinners and saints.
Many people deal with the physical.
If we want to help those in pain, then we will deal with the spiritual.
The hungry need the Bread of Life, the
thirsty need the Water of Life.
Jesus lives within our souls; his love makes us whole.

A stranger in ragged clothing can bring fear.
Do we look away, or draw near?
As we help with the physical, remember the
spiritual. Jesus will clothe the soul.
Sick and a prisoner need Jesus the most. The
body is weak, and sin imprisons the soul.
The body may be healed and set free. Jesus does the same spiritually.

I SEE JESUS

How we treat others, and what we say, will be revealed on that day.
So let our action and our word, reveal Jesus as our Lord.
"Do unto others as you would have them do unto you"
"Whatever you did for these…you did for me"
Speak about Jesus in every way
Tell of his love every day!

(December 14, 2022)

The Longing

The voice was honestly confused, coming from the phone.
Frustration, some anger, seeking truth, feeling all alone.
The words echo in my mind, "Why did God make me this way?"
I prayed for God's help as the voice continued to say,

"Did God make a mistake? Why did he do this to me?"
I knew this person, from child to adult, precious to me.
"I was born this way. Why me? What am I to do?"
My heart was breaking. Father, help me respond with you!

Compassion, sympathy and love filled my heart and mind.
Oh, Holy Spirit, may your words be mine!
Help me speak words that bring Jesus to this soul.
Such confusion; a heart, seeking to be whole!

Partial truth had led to confusion about God.
Things learned as a child rejected as odd.
The worldly standards were so easy to accept.
That day, they were a rope around the neck!

As we talked, the need became clear to me.
Jesus could release a soul from sin's misery!
Sadly, my heart was to be broken.
"Thanks for talking. I must go." The words were spoken.

So much needed said, yet volumes were left unspoken.
I felt so inadequate; but God's love cannot be broken!
I trust God will rescue this seeking One,
God is Love. He will not rest until that soul is won!

(July 11, 2023)

Blindsided

There are times when life is pleasing, and the days seem to have a comfortable feeling that relaxes the mind and soul. Such days tend to arrive in the summer. My maternal grandparents were in Florida with their recreational vehicle. Alfred and Elsie Bennett were on vacation to get away from the weather in Pennsylvania.

From my child's point of view, they had been married for centuries because they were old! I was somewhere around six years old, which explains my perspective.

Grandma had been raised to show respect for her husband. Grandpa was the king. We should not impose our lifestyles on people who were raised with different social standards.

Grandpa loved Grandma and gave her everything she wanted. He was a firm man, but he loved his wife and their children. They had one son and three daughters. He never raised his voice or his hand to any of them. His love was deep, and his words were final.

Grandma loved everyone with hugs, laughter, and an attitude that they were very important people. Her joy was contagious. The house was filled with love and discipline. For example, every meal was conducted the same way. Grandma would have everything on the table, and everyone would stand behind their chairs until Grandpa would enter and stand behind his chair at the head of the table. Everyone would sit down after he sat down. Only after praying for the meal were people allowed to eat. Grandma, however, would always stand up and start fussing over the table. Everyone would tell her to sit down and eat. There was enough food for everyone.

The day started with Grandma making breakfast while Grandpa read the newspaper. After eating, Grandpa returned to the paper as Grandma cleaned the dishes and table. She told Grandpa she was going outside to do something. He mentioned that he didn't feel good, so he was going to stay behind. When she returned, she found him deceased. She ran down the camp's road screaming for help. She was suddenly alone, in Florida, her husband's body sitting in the camper. Finally, she found some help.

It was early morning when our phone rang. Mom and Dad were sleeping in their bed, and I was in my bed. Normally, Mom would answer the phone. That morning was different. Dad knew something was wrong before the first ringing sound faded away. He was out of bed while saying, "I'll get it."

Our apartment was small, and I was just old enough to realize something was wrong, so I stayed in my room. I could hear everything, but I knew Mom and Dad needed to be alone.

Dad was listening to the person on the phone. He told them to hold on. Dad went to Mom and told her the news. I heard Mom's scream and her crying. She got the phone. All I heard was the crying. I was crying too. I didn't understand about death. I was crying because my mom was crying. Dad was her rock that day. Mom came to my room, and we wept together. Eventually, we turned to the Lord in prayer.

We understood that Jesus would be the only one who could take our shattered hearts and restore them. Jesus was the center of our home. We dealt with the funeral, the burial, the family gathering. The Lord was with us.

How often do we realize how much Jesus is always with us? Do we know that we are always on God's mind? Do we turn to the Holy Spirit for his help? Why do we choose to bear the pain alone?

If we take every experience of our lives and add up all the emotions that we felt, then compare that to Jesus Christ on the Cross, we would be humbly amazed at his pain and sacrifice and his love!

Yes, the love of Jesus is the greatest love.

Dear Jesus, I need you. Please forgive me and fill me with your love. In your name, Amen.

(July 19, 2023)

The Old and the New

The Bible was read, devotions were done,
my prayers were said, I was ready to run.
Then I sat down, I had a new thought,
was I thinking and living the way God taught?
I saw the old me, just what I used to be,
I was so awful, it frightened me.
Bitter, senseless, filled with ignorance and grief,
I was so lost, like some brutish beast.

Then I thought of you, holding my hand,
yes, you were there, always present,
To guide and console me into God's Heaven.
My flesh will age, my heart may fail,
but God is my strength, he will prevail.
When I think of Jesus, to consider his worth,
then I have no desire for this old earth.

Alas, the unfaithful, those far away,
are choosing destruction, when they fail to obey,
But, as for me, with Jesus my God,
in him I take refuge, in him I am loved.
My soul is refreshed, my attitude soars,
the old me is gone, the new has come.
My heart does rejoice in Jesus my Lord,
God smiles and says, "Welcome, well done!"

(November 15, 2022)

My Thoughts:

Chapter 4

Adversity

My Skiing Adventure

One year our church youth group decided to go snow skiing. Our group had around ten members. David and his wife, Mary Lou, were young and enjoyed activities, making them excellent youth leaders. We had to have our parents sign a release for the trip. My parents signed reluctantly because my mother was worried about my safety.

We went to a place that had a chalet on top of the hill where visitors parked their cars. It was a Saturday, so it was busy. Two slopes started from a common area on top of the hill. The beginner's slope went to the left while the professional slope went straight ahead. We had the required training before skiing. We were ready to go and have fun.

Most of us went down the beginner's slope first, then we did the professional slope. Some of the group went to the chalet for refreshments. I suddenly found myself alone at the top of the hill. Looking back, I should have gone with the group to the chalet. Standing alone, and since I was now a professional skier, having done both slopes, I decided to tighten the holder screw on my left boot.

Two turns felt snug. I went down the beginner's slope, fell, and broke my leg because the boot did not release. It was a very bad break. I saw some of my friends above me at the chalet. I waved my arms for help, and they waved back! Another skier stopped at my side and asked if I was okay. I knew she was trying to be helpful, but I was lying on the slope with my leg pointing in a very unnatural position. I told her I needed help. A few minutes later, the rescue crew arrived.

The trip to the hospital had two patients in the back of our youth leader's station wagon. My friend Dennis had a sprained ankle, and I had a broken leg. Mary Lou was a nurse, so she took care of us during the hour-long trip to the hospital. The hospital emergency room looked like something on a television show. The waiting room was full, and people were in every room and lined up in the hallway.

I was taken past everyone, right to the front of the line. I still remember their expressions as I rolled past them. I really felt sorry for them.

While I waited for the doctor, I remembered what Mom told me before I left for the skiing trip. She was very worried about me. She was also a very strong woman who had learned to trust God. When she felt powerless to stop something, she would use humor as a final attempt to get others to change their minds. As I was headed out the door, she said in a firm voice, "Don't you come crying home to me with a broken leg!"

Although I was taken to the front of the line, I ended up waiting almost an hour because of another person that arrived from a car accident. Mary Lou stayed with me that whole time. She told me that my parents had been called and would be there soon. When I saw them, Mom had been crying while Dad acted very stoic. I had to do something to make them feel better. With a smile, I said, "Mom, at least I didn't go crying home with a broken leg!" Everyone laughed. The tension was removed, and we all felt better about the situation.

Everyone experiences times of trial and testing. We may cause our own difficulties, or they may be placed upon us. In every situation, we have the ability to be overcomers when we depend on Jesus Christ. The people who depend on Jesus can face the hard times because their hearts belong to Jesus.

God is always taking care of those who love him. Do we face chronic illnesses? Do we struggle financially? Do we have relationship concerns? Does it seem that our spiritual enemy keeps nipping at our heels? As long as we keep Jesus first in our hearts and lives, we can say with Paul,

> Who shall separate us from the love of Christ? Shall trouble or hardship or persecution or famine or nakedness or danger or sword? No, in all these things *we are more than conquerors through him who loved us.* For I am convinced that neither life nor death, neither angels nor demons, neither the present nor the future, nor any powers, neither height nor depth, nor any-

thing else in all creation, will be able to separate
us from the love of God that is in Christ Jesus our
Lord. (Romans 8:35, 37, 38) (Emphasis added)

The ability to overcome is only available through Jesus Christ. *Jesus is the Conqueror!*

As time passed, I ended up with several people standing around the bed. The doctor arrived and told everyone to leave except for my parents and Mary Lou.

He listened to my breathing, started to examine my leg, and said "Hmmm" several times.

I had a feeling he was going to say something very negative, so I said, "Doctor, I can move my toes."

"You can?" was his immediate reply. "Show me."

I wiggled my toes, and a subdued cheer was heard. This was big news since my leg bones had shattered into almost a thousand pieces. He had said there were too many to count.

Eventually, everyone got home. Dennis's ankle healed quickly. My healing took six months. My left leg is over one inch shorter than my right leg.

Should I have asked, "Why me"? Should I have blamed my mom for my injury because she mentioned a broken leg? Should I have brought a lawsuit to the skiing place? Should I have been upset that the hospital was crowded?

What if I just accepted the responsibility since I tightened the holder without getting help? Why do people always try to blame someone for their own sins?

Adam said Eve made him sin. Eve said the serpent made her sin. Jesus wants us to openly admit our failures and sins. He wants us to admit he is the only Savior. He wants us to be overcomers *through* him. No matter what happens to us, Jesus is there to help us through the situation.

Imagine it. Name the worst thing you face in your life. You have two possible ways to view that problem. You can view it as a terrible negative and spend time making it a Goliath that taunts you every day. Or you can offer it up to Jesus. He will make you an overcomer.

He will handle that Goliath by giving you five smooth stones. You know what to do.

God will always be with us. He is the Lord, and nothing is greater that Jesus!

(January 29, 2023)

Who Am I?

There once was a time, just when I can't say,
Things were not fine; I must get away!
People surround me, they are on every side!
They know all the answers, but who am I?

Eat this food, take this pill; get up and move, no, be still.
Bleach your teeth, color your hair.
It's all for your benefit, we really do care!

Then came the day, when "Stop!" was my cry!
Enough from you! Who am I?
And to my surprise, this is no lie, God asked me, Who Am I??
He made me stop, what could I say?
I bowed my head and began to cry.
You are God, but who am I?

Lift up your head, let the tears dry, behold my Love, for you I died!
See the Cross, see the Tomb. I am not there; I am with you!
I am with you, inside your heart.
Wherever you go, whatever you face.
Be of good cheer, I will never depart.
You are my child, you I embrace.

Now I know, just who am I. Jesus gives me my identity.
Saved by Grace, never to die. Thanks to Jesus, I am me!

(November 13, 2022)

Turn Adversity into Victory

Turn adversity into victory, it's easy to say,
But this is life, it can be hard.
So, tell me please, is there a way
What must I do, where do I start
To turn adversity into victory, today.

Before we start, we must stop.
What you ask, and seek, this victory,
We must start with all honesty,
Looking deep within your heart,
To turn adversity into victory, today.

We look deep inside, what do we see?
Do we see all kinds of sin, deep within?
Despair and shame lead to sorrow and fear,
Gossip and grudges dance with darkness and sin.
Only Jesus turns adversity into victory, ask him!

Jesus is God's only Son, his Power beyond measure,
He is the Savior, our Lord and God, our very Treasure.
He faced every adversity, tempted and tried
His blood was shed for our salvation, for us he died.
To turn adversity into victory, the cost he satisfied.

His body was taken from that old Cross
Put in a borrowed tomb, all seemed lost.
Yet on the third day
Jesus could not stay
He turned adversity into victory by rising from the grave!

Whatever we face, whatever the sin or challenge,
No matter how entangled, or the sin most evil,
Ask Jesus to forgive and confess his Name,
You he will love and restore, you he will heal
Your adversity becomes victory in Jesus the Lord!

The Carnival

Every year the traveling carnival would come to town and use the old baseball field located near downtown. They had the standard rides with the usual games and all the foods expected at carnivals. It was a wonderful time to have fun, overeat, and frustrate parents. They arrived with everyone ready for a week of fun, then they were gone.

My story begins the day after the carnival left town. I was around eleven years old. The day was sunny and warm. I told my mom I was going out to play. Back then, a kid could go all over town and be perfectly safe. Cell phones did not exist. The town had a small police force because crime was very low.

I decided to ride my bicycle to the field so I could try to find something that might have been dropped by someone. Some might say I was looking for junk. I considered it to be a treasure hunt. I was alone. I was focused on looking at the ground. I was in trouble.

Sometimes trouble seems to appear out of nowhere. Usually, trouble finds us because we aren't paying attention. Think about it. How would events have been different if we had been more observant? I was not being observant. I was too focused on my own desires rather than seeing what was happening around me. Where is our focus? What are we missing?

I was brought back to reality when three high-school boys surrounded me on their bicycles. I was a big boy physically, but I was still a boy mentally. I was raised to avoid fighting. Violence was not in my nature. If only I had been paying attention *before* I was surrounded!

They started teasing me about my weight. I will not describe everything they did to me. During this event, I saw a guy about two blocks away. I yelled for help but to no avail. By the time they finished, I walked my broken bicycle home with two flat tires. I wasn't in good shape either.

I opened the front door to find my parents sitting there, looking at me. They didn't seem surprised to see me. They had heard about my encounter. They never told me how they knew; they just knew.

We went to the police station. My parents had called them before I was home and told them I would identify the attackers. I didn't know their names, so I described them. The officer nodded his head and said he knew them. They were already repeat offenders.

Now I was getting frightened. I told the officer and my parents that I didn't want any more trouble with those boys. I was reassured that they would not bother me again. I found out later the boys were arrested and sentenced to juvenile detention.

What do we learn from this event? How does this relate to our spiritual lives? Here are some things to consider. I am sure more truth, or lessons, will be found.

God allows us to make our own choices, even if they lead into trouble. Our reasons for our choices may be innocent or not. God can create a positive outcome. Even if we must go through "the valley of the shadow of death," God enables us to declare, "I will fear no evil for thou art with me!"

Children are always cautioned to be careful. Does that include being aware of our surroundings? Walking, driving, serving the Lord, everything requires awareness of our surroundings. We are better witnesses when we are better observers. Does someone seem sad, distracted, worried, confused, or something else? If so, that is an opportunity to be a friend, to spend some time listening, or giving a hug, or speaking encouragement—all of it is an opportunity to bring Jesus into the situation.

Everyone will experience pain and suffering, regardless of the cause. While I was being subjected to abuse, my concern was how my parents would react. I just wanted to let it go. Bruises would heal. Embarrassment would pass with time. Instead, the police were involved. Here is another lesson I learned: parents *do* know what is best for their child. Jesus acknowledged this when he said,

> Which of you fathers, if your son asks for
> a fish, will give him a snake instead? Or if he
> asks for an egg, will give him a scorpion? If you

> then, though you are evil, know how to give good
> gifts to your children, how much more will your
> Father in heaven give the Holy Spirit to those
> who ask him. (Luke 11:11–13)

Parents, God himself is the example of parenthood. Throughout the Bible, his love for us, his children, is found again and again. Although we are imperfect, we love our children. Yes, some people fail to be parents. The reasons are not the point here. The results remain the same. Parents and children live without acknowledging God's love. It is so very important to keep Jesus in the center of our families.

Time passed. I healed physically and mentally. I have no idea what happened with the three boys. It is my prayer that they received the help they needed. I never knew their names. I didn't know their families. I had no idea about their social status. So they are in the hands of God's Only Son, Jesus Christ.

Our final lesson is compassion. When we are treated evilly, we can't focus on evil; we must have compassion.

> Blessed are you when people insult you,
> persecute you and falsely say all kinds of evil
> against you because of me. Rejoice and be glad,
> because great is your reward in heaven, for in the
> same way they persecuted the prophets who were
> before you. (Matthew 5:11–12)

There is always something to learn from the experiences of our lives. The Lord is pleased when we learn more about him. Imagine how much family lives would be affected if they took time every day to share an event and discuss how God loved them.

I did find a small trinket that day. I don't remember it, nor do I know whatever happened to it. It doesn't matter. What matters is my relationship with Jesus and my relationship with others. Thank you, Jesus, for loving me!

(April 1, 2023)

A New Life

I have often heard about the man called Jesus
People sing, pray and teach that he saves us,
All that I know is my own story
A hard life of pain and sorrow, and no glory.

My life has no meaning, I'm like a ship lost at sea,
The waves beat me and toss me about,
The storms of life rage at me
Fear and agony rule my heart, my mind is full of doubt.

I look for an answer, but where do I start?
Drink? Drugs? Lust? Crime? Where is my heart?
These things are traps destroying me deep inside.
Now, a new thought for me; Jesus, here am I!

Yes, I really mean it, Jesus, I mean it for real.
Take my sins away from me, I ask you to heal.
I make my declaration, public is my cry,
Every sin, deep within, you took from me at Calvary!

Now I live free, my sins are all gone.
The love of Jesus for me, is greater than every sin.
My life is now his, and his life is now mine,
Oh, the joy I feel now that I have God's love!

I am so glad that I heard about Jesus.
I sing, and pray, and teach that he saves us.
All that I know is my own story,
A new life in Jesus of praise and glory!

(November 22, 2022)

Cancer

Stop reading.
Speak the word as you see fit.
Scream it, *CANCER*!
Whisper it, cancer.
Speak with seething hatred, C-A-N-C-E-R!
Go ahead. I will wait.

What you are going to read is true. This is as accurate as possible a report of how my mother, Doloris Decker, dealt with her cancer. (Her name is spelled correctly.) It is my prayer that her story will encourage the reader as they deal with the way cancer affects them.

Prediscovery

Cancer is rapidly growing cells. They grow so rapidly that the body can't deal with them. They overwhelm other cells. They are not invaders. They come from your own body. Here is the first question: Why did this happen to me? Did I do something to make this happen? Did I eat the wrong things? Think of a million questions, and there is only one answer: *no*.

These questions are based on the premise that the person with the cancer did, or didn't, do something to cause the cancer. Such thoughts only serve to discourage, confuse, and mislead. The same applies to those who insist cancer is caused by heredity. Somebody, somewhere, somehow, developed a defective gene to make you have cancer.

Every such scenario leads into the hands of our spiritual enemy. What serves Satan better, a confused mind or a mind focused on Jesus?

Discovery

Obviously, I was not there when Dodie (my mother's daily name) discovered the first bump. Over the years, she shared with me what she was doing and her feelings. I will be very careful to report accurately her story.

Dodie stood alone looking in the mirror. Her left hand was touching the lump that she could not see. Perhaps she was wrong. After all, the skin was clear. She kept looking and looking. As the tears slipped down her face, she accepted the truth. She had been subject to skin cancer for years. She would go to the doctor, have it removed, and return to her life. It was no big deal. Not now. This was going to be a big deal. She just knew it. She couldn't stand there all day. Things had to be done. She finished dressing, dried her tears, and opened the door. She would walk through the door of faith to face her future with Jesus.

At the time, I had no idea what was happening with my mom. She told my dad and my grandparents. I am sure she told other family members. It would be years later that I would learn everything Dodie had to handle. They felt it was not my place to know about things that affected a woman's body. That was their choice and their right as my parents. They didn't understand that I was aware of breast cancer.

Children are aware of things that happen to their parents. Parents should consider telling their children about cancer. They know more than you think. My parents wanted to protect me. Their one blind spot was not wanting me to grow up. I was old enough to know what Mom was facing.

Sharing

Very few can really understand what the woman endures. The body is fighting itself. The immune system tries to destroy the cancer cells that are trying to destroy them. The chemical balances are affected, causing emotional distress. Some women deal with changes to monthly occurrences.

Then it is time to share with others. The well-meaning really have no idea how to respond.

"Oh, nooo!"

"I'm sooo sorry!"

How should one respond?

You may feel like screaming, "Enough! Doesn't anyone understand?"

Paul encourages to respond, "Therefore, as God's chosen people, holy and dearly loved, clothe yourselves with compassion, kindness, humility, gentleness and patience" (Colossians 3:12).

Try to understand that people are trying to be helpful and sympathetic. They honestly care about you and find themselves struggling to express themselves. Although it might not seem fair, God wants the person who is ill to wear compassion, kindness, humility, gentleness, and patience. When the one with cancer loves others enough to understand the other person's situation, then both people will find God gives them peace.

Sharing becomes the first step of healing. Sharing helps us to step beyond our own problems. It helps us to invest in others. A shared pain is less painful. Even better, when friends and you worship together, pray together, and invite Jesus to join you, the door is opened for God to bless you as only he can bless you.

Confronting Reality

Dodie discovered her cancer was worse than she expected. It had spread into the lymph nodes. Today, such cancer is usually cured with minimal surgery. Dodie faced a far different future. Radical mastectomy. The removal of the entire right breast with the lymph nodes from the chest wall, through the shoulder, and down into the right arm. The only words I could use to describe her were "hollowed out." It was sad, very sad.

She had to wear a prosthetic device to look "normal."

She was in her forties when the cancer struck. She lost so much. Yet she kept her faith in God as the center of her life. From the outside, she moved on. The healing process was much slower inside. The years rolled past, and the Lord helped her heal. My best guess for the time that passed was twenty years.

Then the cancer returned. She lost her left breast. My dad passed away in 2000. She spent another decade living by herself. I don't know the details of those years. I do know that she was at total peace with her life. She had a very strong relationship with the Lord. During those years, she continued to have skin cancer. Dodie went to heaven in 2016. She was eighty-nine years old. She was less than three months away from ninety.

An Unexpected Epilogue

My mom, Dodie, had learned over the years that trusting the Lord was more than just something to say. *Trusting the Lord is a living relationship that is based in the love of Jesus Christ and is nourished by the Holy Spirit for the glorification of God.* (Read that sentence again.)

Even though she went through so much pain, and so much loss, she was filled with the joy of salvation! Much to my chagrin and embarrassment, in her later years, she stopped wearing her devices. She even started telling people, while laughing, "I don't have any boobies!" She had so much joy that everyone would laugh *with* her! No, they did not laugh at her. They laughed *with* her!

I will not minimize what people experience with cancer. (I am a cancer survivor. I know firsthand what I experienced.) Your experiences are real and valid. How they are handled is where you will experience the incredible love of God. Satan wants you to be discouraged, fearful, angry, lonely, and impatient. Please choose to live in Jesus's love as offered at Calvary and the empty tomb.

Jesus said, "I tell you the truth, whoever hears my word and believes him who sent me has eternal life and will not be condemned; he has crossed over from death to life" (John 5:24).

Have you asked Jesus to forgive your sins? Please do ask him.

A prayer:

> Father God, I am terrified. I have heard so many
> stories. I don't know what to think or do. My
> emotions are a mess. Do I laugh or cry? I feel like

a ship caught in a huge storm. Jesus, I am tired of being alone. I am grateful for everyone who tries to help me. Thank you for them. But I need you, Lord. This is going to be hard. Please take away my fear. Help me to trust you. Calm my nerves. Build my faith in you and in others. Stay with me throughout my cancer. Let my story be one that will glorify you and encourage others. Help me, today, tomorrow, forever. I love you. In Jesus's name, Amen.

(April 28, 2023)

Joyous Surrender

When the world has you down,
When you need to be found,
Hear the Lord's cry,
Here am I! Here am I!

Give me your love, give me your burdens.
Give me your heart, give me your sins.
Look at my Cross and see how I die.
I am Salvation! Here am I!

Sin has been conquered.
The tomb is empty.
Christ is alive!
I am Risen! Here am I!

Here am I! Here am I!
Rejoice and sing, "Glorify!"
Sing of God's love!
Sing of God's Son!

Jesus our Savior,
What he has done!
How should we reply?
Here am I! Here am I!

What work can be done?
At home or away?
What need can I find?
To say, here am I?

REV. ALFRED L. DECKER

Open my heart to Jesus's heart.
Open my mind to his mind.
Open my arms like his arms.
Open my Soul to Jesus's Soul.

He says to me, here am I!
From cradle to Cross, here am I!
From tomb to my Throne, here am I!
From creation to eternity, here am I!

Let our praises rise!
Let us glorify!
God says to us: Here am I!
We say to God: Here am I!

(May 2, 2023)

More Than an Accident

The Lord understands what we need long before we even realize the need for ourselves. Therefore, he is proactive when it comes to our yet unknown needs. God starts working on our behalf so when we recognize we have a need, the answer is already prepared.

Our youth leader when I was a teenager was a young man named David. His wife was named Mary Lou. David was a PK, a preacher's kid. His love for Jesus and his family helped to make him the best youth leader we ever had in our little church.

David was an engineer at a firm that made single-engine airplanes. He was the guy who figured out how to take all those small parts, put them together, and have a plane that flew. He was so dedicated to safety that he personally flew every plane before the customer was allowed to purchase the plane.

He was also avid about his motorcycle. It was a big machine with plenty of room for two adults. It rumbled with power. David could handle it; he was our youth leader. He was young, strong, and very intelligent. He was in love with Jesus and lived like everyone was the most important person in his life.

Then David had a very bad accident while riding his motorcycle. The result of the accident was his right hand was caught on the chain and was mutilated by going around the sprocket. The damage was traumatic. The church, our youth group, and hundreds of others were in fervent prayer for David.

The local hospitals recommended specialized care that would require David going to Philadelphia. That would require almost seven hours' driving time, renting a hotel room for a week, and driving home for the weekend. There had to be another way to get to Philadelphia. Of course! He would fly! He spent several months flying to Philadelphia three days a week while managing to keep working and be home every night to tuck the children into bed. Eventually,

David was released from medical care. His hand was saved, with only the little finger left with some damage.

> So do not fear, for I am with you; do not be
> dismayed, for I am your God. I will strengthen
> you and help you; I will uphold you with my
> righteous right hand. (Isaiah 41:10)

Do not fear. Satan uses fear to influence us. He tries to control us with fear. What does God say? I am with you! I am your God! Don't be afraid, I will strengthen you! I will help you! In fact, I will uphold you! Just hold on to my righteous right hand. Did you know that God has a "righteous right hand"? His name is Jesus! While Jesus is in heaven, we have the Holy Spirit who helps us to live pleasing to God.

> And he who searches our hearts knows the
> mind of the Spirit, because the Spirit intercedes
> for the saints in accordance with God's will. And
> we know that in all things God works for the
> good of those who love him, who have been called
> according to his purpose. (Romans 8:27–28)

God did not make David have an accident. However, God was prepared should David have an accident. *God loves us more than we can imagine!*

(June 20, 2023)

Praise God

Our Heavenly Father, Creator of all things,
To you we give our worship and adoration.
For your glory we play music and sing.
We declare your majesty over every nation.

We rejoice in your only Son, our Lord Jesus Christ.
Jesus loved us before we ever knew about him.
Crucified, buried, and risen, he gives eternal life.
Bow to our Savior and praise the Lord in Heaven!

We are grateful for your Holy Spirit.
He knows your thoughts and your heart.
He teaches us about you, and we believe it!
God, you are amazing! How great thou art!

Your power and authority leave us in awe.
Your will is done in your creation.
Jesus reveals to us our incredible God.
Jesus will be glorified by every nation!

Precious Lord, how well you understand us!
Made in your Image; with faith, hope and love.
Your Divine Love gave us our Lord Jesus!
We glorify and praise you, both here and above!

(January 7, 2024)

The Six-Inch Nail

There was a sense of excitement mixed with fellowship coming from the people scattered around the yard behind the house. The morning dew was gone, showing that the grass had not been cut. The length of the grass was ignored by everyone. The weather was gorgeous! It was a perfect fall day!

The activity in the yard centered on the large copper kettle placed between the house and the church next door. The kettle stood above the firepit where the wood logs were burning. The people of the church were enjoying the fellowship and excitement of anticipation. It was apple butter day!

Laughter seemed to leap from one person to another. Snippets of hymns could be heard rising to God in heaven. They wafted upward with the sweet aroma of fresh, hot apple butter.

The glass canning jars were washed, ready to hold the fruit of our labors. This was an annual activity for the congregation of the small church I pastored. Since it was a Saturday, most of the congregation was helping with the work. Those who had other obligations tried to spend some time with us too.

I had been on stirring duty. Apple butter required constant stirring to cook properly, so everyone took turns "stirring the pot," as we jokingly called that task. I had been stirring for a while and was glad when my replacement arrived. I was ready for a drink of lemonade. As I turned to walk away, I felt an unusual pain in my right foot. Looking down, I saw an old, rusted, dirty six-inch nail sticking out of the top of my shoe!

All I could focus on was the nail poking out of my shoe. I gave no thought to the beautiful day, or the sweet smell of fresh apple butter, or the people staring at me. The nail had my attention.

What was I thinking at that moment? Before that can be answered I need to explain my background. I was raised not to swear, curse, or use any words that were vulgar. The longer I have served

Jesus, the easier it has become to maintain God's standard for speech. Although no one is perfect, God is pleased when we try our best to live like Jesus.

A wise person told me to do the following if I felt that I had failed the Lord: *admit* the failure, *ask* his forgiveness, *accept* his love as well as the consequences of the failure, and *advance* in the way of holiness. This works.

After a moment of looking at my foot, my mind acknowledged that my foot needed medical care. That was when the pain finally hit me. I had been injured many times as a child, so I knew enough to leave the nail in my foot and to keep my foot off the ground. By this time several people were close enough to hear me when I spoke in a calm voice, "God bless me. I've stepped on a nail!" One man standing beside me said, "Aren't you gonna' cuss, or nuthin'?"

The people were amazed at my behavior. I wonder why? Is it acceptable to praise God when the same mouth speaks vulgarities or says bad things about someone?

Jesus spoke clearly and with absolute authority:

> But I tell you that men will have to give account on the day of judgment for every careless word they have spoken. For by your words, you will be acquitted, and by your words you will be condemned. (Matthew 12:36, 37)

I was taken for medical care, my foot healed, and everyone enjoyed the apple butter. Hopefully, more people will live as Jesus taught us to live. Shall we start today?

(August 16, 2023)

Go or Stay

Good morning, my friend, I'm so very glad to meet you!
Thank you for answering my knock on your door.
There is much to get done; Oh, you ask me, who are you?
We should sit down. I am God, it's true. I will tell you more.

I am here to help you understand me.
I am all powerful, far beyond what people think of me.
I am love, pure divine love. My love is what you need.
So, I decided to reveal myself as three.

My name is "I Am" because I am me!
I know this may be hard, but "I Am" is three.
You call me God the Father and that is who I am.
"I Am" also my Son, Jesus Christ, and my Son is also "I Am" me!

People need me to be God, the final authority.
Jesus is me, my Word, my Love, the Lamb of Calvary.
My love for you is so deep, I gave my only Son.
He died and rose again; yes, we are one.

Then there is my Holy Spirit, he is also me.
He knows me more than anyone, except for my Son.
Perhaps you've heard that I made you like me,
My friend, you are also three in one!

Body, mind and soul, some say body, soul and spirit.
The words do not matter, the concept is the same.
You are more than just a body, more than the physical,
You are a living soul that has a spirit; we are the same.

I SEE JESUS

Let me help you understand, here is what we will do.
I am God, I am the Holy Spirit, and I am the Son.
Each of us has our own ministry; thus, we are three,
Each ministry always returns to our unity of One!

Creation will teach you about me as three.
Since I am God, what I did was say, "Let there be…"
Then Jesus, my Living Word, acted to make it happen,
As my Holy Spirit gave them breath, so it was complete!

Here we sit, my friend, one trinity to another.
As Father, Son, and Spirit, I am in love with you!
Let me ask, do you love me, too?
Will you tell me you love me? Nothing else will do.

"I Am" God the Father. I am your salvation.
"I Am" the Holy Spirit, "I Am" Jesus the Lord.
"I Am" here for you. Together, you and me.
What do you say? Should I go or should I stay?

(December 20, 2022)

"I Hate You"

It was sometime during the latter half of the nineteen seventies. I don't recall the exact year. Diane and I were living in eastern Pennsylvania. Her family lived in the area, and since she had been raised in that area, she thought it would be a good place to begin her teaching career.

In the meantime, I was looking for a job that would not endanger my life. Endanger my life? Let me explain.

The first job I found was at a factory where they ground chunks of wax into a very fine powder. They also processed various chemical compounds. Those employees had to wear respirators. I had to wear a face mask. Every day I would go home covered in a fine white powder. Within days, I developed a cough. Near the end of my first month, another crew spent their day processing a red-colored wax. That night I started coughing up red powder. I notified the company of my immediate resignation.

Working as a clerk at a gas station wasn't much better. After a fellow worker was robbed, my wife insisted that I resign to find another job. That led to cleaning an egg-processing plant. An older building had been used for grading and processing thousands of eggs every day. Have you ever tried to pick up an egg outside of the shell? Now imagine a factory with hundreds of broken eggs everywhere. It was a very dirty, slippery job. We were constantly falling. That was another job I resigned.

Finally, I was hired as a supervisor for a company that cleaned factories and their offices. I was assigned to five factories with a total crew of twenty employees. My boss took me around the first day to meet the people and for my orientation. This process went quite well except for one man. Imagine my surprise when he looked at me and said, "I hate you!" I just stood there, too shocked to move. I slowly turned to my boss, but he was also shocked.

The man stood there, his hands clutching a mop handle, shaking with anger. My boss started giving him a warning. He expected everyone to treat me with respect. He immediately gave him a two-word reply, "I quit!" He dropped the mop handle and walked out! My boss apologized and assured me that I was not the cause of that man's behavior. I felt sorry for that man.

Why had he hated me? We had never met before that day. I forgave him even though I would never see him again. I told my boss, who told the owner, that I had forgiven the man. That became a witness to many people.

Jesus wants us to forgive anyone who treats us unjustly.

"But I tell you, love your enemies and pray for those who persecute you, so that you may be children of your Father in heaven," Jesus said in Matthew 5:44, 45. When it comes to forgiveness, Jesus said in Matthew 18:22 that we should forgive "seventy times seven," or 490 times, for the same offense!

They may say they hate us, but we are expected to live like Jesus and tell them that Jesus loves them and so do we, so we forgive them. Is there someone you need to forgive? Do you need someone to forgive you?

Dear God, thank you for loving us and giving us your Son to be our Lord and Savior. He died and rose again for the forgiveness of our sins. May we also be people who forgive! In Jesus's name, Amen.

(December 8, 2023)

A Little Sleep

"Once upon a time" or "I remember when,"
Words to tell a story or a time to begin.
Be it a simple rhyme or a grand, epic tale,
It must have a moral and be told quite well.

I was raised to be busy, much needed done.
I had responsibilities, chores first, then fun.
As I grew older my duties became a time trap,
Feeling overwhelmed, I started to nap.

My dad was good at napping, a regular champ.
He could sleep anytime, anywhere; king of the nap.
But I see things another way, thus I say,
Naps are fine, but not by me, I want to stay awake.

The time is short, the harvest is ripe.
Are the workers prepared or do they say, "good night"?
God does not slumber, nor does he sleep.
God does not need rest, but I do need sleep.

God made the day, and he made the night.
I must work during the day and sleep at night.
Then napping will be foreign to me,
I want to be awake when Jesus comes for me!

Let me be found when the trumpet I hear,
Doing the work of my Father so dear.
I want to see Jesus with my eyes opened wide.
I want to look upon him, since it was for me, he died!

I SEE JESUS

Yes, I am human, and a nap may happen.
Yet I will strive to be awake and not napping.
I see the harvest; the work is undone.
I will sleep later, after I hear God say, "Well done!"

(January 15, 2023)

My Thoughts:

Chapter 5

The Seeking

Determined or Hardheaded?

These stories are true. They are also very funny. My grandmother lived in a small town in Western Pennsylvania. These stories happened in the late 1970s. The small town was built on the side of a mountain. The valley area held a river and some industries. The road in the valley hosted all the government buildings and the entertainment establishments.

The rest of the houses were built with the front door level to the street while the backs had two floors. Grandma's garage was an old, wooden structure supported with concrete blocks and bricks that were randomly stacked together. Two double doors opened outward. An old tree stood to the left side of the garage. That tree had a steel cable fastened to it and was fastened to the garage to make sure it wouldn't fall!

Grandma was a very determined woman. She was a widow who thoroughly enjoyed making her own decisions. My parents had moved in with her because she was reaching that age when she wasn't as independent as she thought.

One day she didn't tell anyone she was going to the store. She took the car and returned to my parents and her son, who were waiting to have a talk with her. She was not able to drive safely, and they had received phone calls from people who knew her. They politely, but gently, informed her that she was no longer allowed to drive.

It didn't take long for Grandma to take the keys and go to the garage. She had the doors open and was in the car before my dad stopped her. That night my parents and my uncle decided to disconnect the car battery.

Once again, Grandma took the keys and got to the car. When it would not start, she opened the hood, connected the battery, and took off! The family finally realized there was only one way to stop Grandma. My uncle removed the battery and hid it from Grandma!

They decided to let her take the keys and go to the car. They approached her after she had opened the hood to find the battery was gone! She finally got the message. Her driving days were over. She had to accept that her family would gladly drive her to the store.

Love is always willing and available to keep others safe. Two different times the disciples were in a boat and were afraid of a severe storm. Both times Jesus stepped up to keep them safe. Can we do any less? Adults must take care of the children. Spouses must take care of each other. Adult children must take care of their parents.

Love, sometimes, must be firm. Not cruel, not hard, but firm. Jesus bore our sins and punishment at Calvary. He suffered more than we could ever imagine. Jesus even had to endure separation from God! Jesus willingly suffered, died, and rose again because he loves us! Have we ever tried to think what God must have been experiencing as his Only Son fulfilled the salvation of his creation? God's love had to be firm, even with Jesus. Our salvation depended on the fulfillment of God's love.

My grandma accepted her new role as passenger. Family members always took her to the stores. She took her final trip when she was eighty-nine. She left behind an empty garage held up by a steel cable.

Just three houses away from my grandma lived two sisters. They were twins who lived together to share expenses in their senior years. They were very sweet ladies who treated everyone with respect and dignity. Their house was well kept and filled with mementoes of the past.

Visiting them was guaranteed to be a pleasant experience of hospitality, pleasant conversation, and plenty of laughs. Yes, they really completed each other's sentences! They were very precious, so this historical event is offered with the greatest of love and respect. Although both have died, I will call them Bessie and Tessie.

Bessie had been slowly losing her vision while Tessie was slowly going deaf. Everyone in town knew the sisters and would gladly do anything for them. Like my grandma, they were very determined to be independent. Their attitude would lead them to their last adventure with driving.

It was a pleasant summer day. Bessie and Tessie loved being outdoors. They relied on each other to remain independent. They decided to drive the three blocks to the local grocery store.

Bessie was the driver. Tessie was the navigator. Tessie had a problem because she never learned to drive. And Bessie was legally blind! Their threeblock drive turned into a weaving, wandering epic adventure suitable for a comedic movie.

Bessie would shout for directions so Tessie could hear her. Tessie would shout back at her to go left or right because she was weaving all over the road. This led them into going all over the town.

Eventually, a policeman pulled them over, only to discover a blind woman driving with a deaf woman giving directions! He took them home without any charges. The car was confiscated until it was sold.

The Lord watched over these sweet ladies that day. No one was hurt, and nothing was damaged. We need each other. No matter how independent we are, we will always need other people. Our Lord didn't settle for just twelve followers, he wanted everyone! John's vision of heaven reports,

> I looked and there before me was a great multitude that no one could count, from every nation, tribe, people and language standing before the throne and in front of the Lamb. (Revelation 7:9)

Determined or hardheaded? Are they different? Yes. Hardheaded is a closed mind where things must be done "my" way. It is a hardness that easily crosses into cruelty. Being determined means being open to new ideas that wisely and gently reveal to others their need for salvation.

The more we help each other, the more we obey Jesus. It is good that we take time to laugh. Heaven is a place of eternal joy. Jesus is preparing heaven for us that we will have joy.

May we be blessed as we strive to do God's will. May we be a blessing to others. Finally, keep the joy of Jesus in your heart and on your face. Nothing irritates Satan more than a joyful Christian! Let me know the next time you go shopping…I'll drive! There *is* joy in the Lord!

(March 19, 2023)

Praise His Name

What does it take to listen to God?
What must he do to get our attention?
Doesn't it seem rather odd,
That we don't seem to know his intentions?

We have free will and independence.
We are free to make our own way.
We may struggle or take a firm stance,
Our results will be what we say.

We go through a life of struggle.
We scurry around like mice in a maze.
Our companions are sorrow and trouble.
When will we listen to God's amazing Grace?

God's Grace is his Son Jesus!
He is our Savior and the Christ.
He died and rose to claim us.
Only Jesus can give eternal life!

Why are we so stubborn?
Why do we want our own way?
Why do we reject the "Firstborn"?
Jesus declared, "I am the way!"

Now is the time for submission.
To soften our hearts to Jesus.
He is ready to forgive our sin.
His is the power to save us!

Let us seek his Holy Will.
Each day to know him better.
Let us pause in prayer, our minds be still,
As we read the Bible, God's love letter.

It is time to focus on our Lord,
To live as he leads us.
Let us trust his every word!
Praise his Holy Name: Jesus! Jesus!

(November 19, 2023)

What Was I Thinking?

Once upon a time a beautiful princess with flowing blond hair married an incredibly handsome prince with dimples and blue eyes. They had a son who was loved by everyone.

Stop! Here is the real story.

Alvin met Doloris (the name is spelled correctly). They got married and had one child, me. I am sure they asked each other after my birth, "What was I thinking!" Trust me when I tell you, I was a handful! During my lifetime, my parents lived in houses and apartments. Mom and Dad lived with my grandma. They lived in a "high-rise" for seniors. After Dad went to heaven, my mom lived in my house, then in a nursing home. No matter where we lived, we lived in a home. *The best home is where people love each other and love Jesus.*

Does this rule out our emotions, our hopes and dreams, our spiritual and social lives? Not at all. When people truly love each other, that love will hold firm, even through the deepest hurts and sufferings. In Acts 7:60, Stephen prays for the people stoning him, "Lord, do not hold this sin against them." Since Stephen loved them so much, shouldn't we love our own family members the same way? We forgive to be forgiven. To be forgiven, we must forgive.

I required a lot of forgiveness when I was a kid. I did not intend to disobey. It wasn't my goal to be bad. I was just a boy who kept busy. Sometimes trouble found me. Mostly trouble was my companion because I didn't bother to think!

One day a friend and I were throwing pieces of broken porcelain. It just so happened that I was throwing a triangular-shaped piece. When I threw it, my hand was cut open. I got on my bike and rode home, walked through the house to the kitchen, bleeding profusely. Mom was washing dishes. I placed my hand directly in front of her eyes and said, "Look!" After the initial shock, we were on the way to the emergency room.

There was another friend, on another day, where we stood on opposite street corners throwing rocks at each other! He won when his rock made the top of my head bleed. Mom wasn't very surprised. Just another trip to the emergency room. My adventures included times when I didn't get hurt too.

There is an old joke that has many versions. I like this version: my mom never had any stupid kids, just me! My parents would get my report card and tell me I could do better. If I wanted to get ahead in life, I would study harder. Occasionally, Mom would get upset and accuse me of using my head for a hat rack! I was a kid. I didn't think about the future. I had good grades in subjects I enjoyed, and average grades in other subjects. Let me say it now—they were right! I should have studied more!

If you are in school, study! Especially the Bible! The Lord wants us to be followers who read the Bible. As Paul wrote to Timothy, "Study to show yourself approved" (2 Timothy, chapter 3).

One day Mom gave me money to buy a loaf of bread and a letter to mail. I went to the mailbox and dropped the money inside! What could I do? I was in trouble! I went home and told Mom what happened and apologized. She gently told me it was all right. Then she asked me what I was going to do! That wasn't fair! She was supposed to give me the solution! I thought about it and decided to wait for the mailman, tell him what I did, get back my money, then go buy the bread. The mailman laughed about my mess and gave me my money.

I am sixty-nine years old. You know what? It is true. It pays to think! Here is my closing advice: learn everything you can learn. Read all types of books. Especially study the Bible. Read commentaries. Read a dictionary. Borrow books from the library and your pastor. I recommend reading books written by the leaders of the early church of God.

Try reading the Bible like any other book. Read it without stopping to ask questions. The idea is to show yourself the overall flow of history. After that, read it slower for study. By the way, my parents were pleased to call me their son. Someday, I pray that God will tell me, "Well done, my son!"

(April 12, 2023)

The Eternal Question

I have a question, said my friend,
What does it mean, to be "born again"?
Here was the question than has no end,
The answer is in Jesus's resurrection!

"I am the way," said Jesus. "I am the truth."
"I am the life," said he; Jesus is our proof!
God so loves us; he gave his Only Son.
He is our Salvation and Resurrection!

There is no mystery in being "born again."
It is placing our faith only in him!
Tell Jesus every failure and sin,
Then believe! And you will be "born again"!

Do you believe what Jesus had said and done?
Are you willing to ask Jesus, God's Only Son,
To forgive your every sin?
Are you ready to be "born again"?

Now is the time. Here is the Son!
I am sorry, Jesus, for all I have done.
Please love me and forgive every sin!
Oh, praise God! I Am "born again"!!

(April 23, 2023)

He Is Greater Than Me

Life. What does it mean to be alive?
Is it day by day filled with strife?
Is there more than just my agony?
Is there a world beyond the one called me?

Why is my world so very small?
I feel safer with me, and that's all.
All that I do is done for me.
I am the only one that I must please.

You should be grateful for all I do.
I am responsible for myself and you!
I keep every moment tightly controlled.
It is my duty, my burden, to keep us whole.

Here is my secret; listen well.
What I do is meant to keep us out of Hell!
If I should fail in any way,
The world itself would pass away!

The burden is great, but one I must carry.
It is my duty. I must not grow weary.
No one else can do what I do.
Do not worry, I will get us through!

What is it you are telling me?
Who do you say can set me free?
Don't you understand anything I said?
Without me the world would be dead!

I SEE JESUS

How dare you say that I am wrong?
How can I be weak? I am the one who is strong!
Who is this one you call Jesus the Lord?
Why do you call him God's Living Word?

What do you mean, he rose from the grave?
That I should believe and not be afraid?
That Jesus loves me for who I am?
That Jesus is the Son of God and Man?

You don't seem to comprehend.
If I stop my duties the world will end!
No one else can handle my duties, none dares!
These are my burdens and my source of despair.

Can Jesus help me, too? Does he really care?
Can he free me from myself? Does he dare?
You call it faith. Me? I am afraid.
Will I lose all the progress I've made?

You must understand what you ask of me.
I am so tired of everyone depending on me.
Will you tell me what to say?
Will you help me find Jesus today?

God, it's me. Don't get me wrong.
I am very tired. It's hard to get along.
I need your help right away.
Will Jesus come now, without delay?

Wait! What is happening to me?
My burden is gone! Where can it be?
I don't have to do those things!
I am free! Free to live for Christ, my King!

REV. ALFRED L. DECKER

I must tell everyone about Jesus Christ!
Believe me! He has given me a new life!
I am free from the sin that defined me!
Thank you, Jesus! I am free!

(December 23, 2023)

My Priority

On Sunday morning I take time to worship.
I go to church and sing songs of praise,
I give some money and I bow my head to pray.
I am a model Christian when I go to Church.

Time for lunch, boy, am I starving!
Forgot to say grace, God understands.
The drive through line needs to keep moving,
I still need to get my shopping done.

The stores were so crowded, I could hardly move.
Great! My child just got sick in the back seat.
The police car has flashing lights on me.
The pressure is building; I better watch what I say and do!

The tire blew out a mile from home; my child has the flu.
The dog stained my new wall-to-wall rug.
From bad to worse, the basement is flooded, too!
I am so overwhelmed! I really need a hug!

The Pastor talked about Colossians 3:17:
Whatever I do, in word or deed,
Do it all in the Name of Jesus, giving thanks
to God the Father through him.
Much to my shame, I think Jesus loves me more than I love him!

Dear Jesus, hear my words and know my heart.
Teach me to praise you in all I do!
Father, take my life and give me a pure heart.
Teach me to live for, and in, you!

No matter how busy my life can be, you
have the ability to change me.
I give you my life and all that I do,
while you give me a new life in you!

Teach me to keep you first in my day,
make it my joy to study and pray.
Show me that worship is my daily urge,
not just something I do in Church.
Whatever I do, in word or in deed,
I do it all in Jesus's name.
He is first in me, my priority.
My life is his, I am born again!

(November 28, 2022)

The Not-So-Empty Chair

I've heard about a judgment day; where some go left, some go right.
As we lived so God will separate; have we lived in his Light?
I know that God is Love, and fair to everyone.
I had nothing to fear; after all, what had I done?

Let me think, let me see; Oh, yes, oh, no; not those memories.
I was a kid, the carnival was in town, I just had to see!
I snuck on the rides, I took a toy; it was all fun, no harm done.
Then I was a teen caught on a joy ride;
it was fun, but harm was done.

Soon some new friends found me; I guess I should have known.
Cigarettes, then drink, weed was my thing, my pain had grown.
My life became a blur, a hazy nightmare; a sad future for me.
Arrested, withdrawal, agony and shame; what had I done, why me?

Sometime later, who knows when? On parole, now join a group.
I found a group at a church, Okay, I'll go, let's just get through!
There was always one empty chair and that made me question,
Why is it here, why was it empty?
The answer led to my redemption!

There was a man, years ago, who was found guilty of a crime.
He was whipped, beaten, tortured, and spat on many times.
He was innocent, but that didn't matter to them.
They wanted him dead and buried, that innocent man.

I was outraged, anger burned in my heart!
How dare they be so evil? Boy, was I hot!
Then the leader softly told me, that man died for you.
I said, what do you mean? I am so confused!

That man is named Jesus, Jesus the Christ, God's Only Son.
He died on the Cross of Calvary, to save everyone.
He rose from the tomb and is now glorified in Heaven.
Do you want his love? Will you accept what he has given?

The truth of Jesus sunk in; I wept bitter tears.
What had I done? So, so many wasted years!
Jesus took my old ways and gave me a new start.
Forgiven and loved; a new me with a new heart!

My friend, will you join me there?
There is now a second chair.
One is beside me, waiting for you.
The other is for Jesus, he is there, too!

(December 13, 2022)

Stay!

There is a war raging inside of me; yes, no, stay, go.
What should I do, what should I be? Away! Away! No, just stay.
Away, away, please go away! I must not listen to what you say.
Away, away, please go away! I must not, I will not, what did you say?

Why do I listen to what you say? I must not give in, please go away.
The struggle is daily, day after day. Away! Away! Oh, just stay.
Then I heard a new cry, it was far away.
A new voice to me, what did he say?
You are not alone, hear me today,
come unto me, I will take you away.

You know where to find me, look this way.
It is Calvary, what do you see?
See the tomb, the stone rolled away.
I am right here, what will it be?
Away! Away! Or should I stay?

Stay! Stay! It's all I can say! Take each of my sins. Away! Away!
You give me peace, joy and love, Jesus my Savior, the Son of God!
The war is gone inside of me, Jesus, is my victory!
Now I know what to say!
Jesus, my Jesus. Stay! Stay!

(November 10, 2022)

My Thoughts:

Chapter 6

Calvary

Gone but Not Forgotten

Most of my school years were spent living in a second-floor apartment. The front door opened to the right, blocking the door to the bathroom. The bathroom was just large enough to hold a tub with four claw-shaped feet. To the left of the living room was my bedroom. It was eight-by-ten feet in size, with a small window in the corner of the ceiling that opened onto the hallway.

The living and dining rooms formed one large area, except there was carpet in the living room. Entering the apartment placed the television on the hallway wall to the left of the door. A loveseat served as our sofa with a rocking chair to the right side. The dining room held the table, a small freezer, and a cabinet. The floor was sloped, so I could push a toy car into the dining room, and it would roll back to me in the living room! My parents' bedroom was to the right of the dining room, and the kitchen was to the left of the dining room.

I am trying to show that my parents were humble people who were thankful to God for a place to live. They did not have great wealth. They had great faith! They demonstrated total reliance upon God for their every need. They had great love! They lived every day for Jesus, to raise me to believe in Jesus for myself. They lived the Great Commission! I will be eternally grateful that God gave me such wonderful parents.

The attic on the third floor was the designated storage area for the tenants. Each area was surrounded with chicken wire. One day I discovered three toys had been stolen: my Lionel train set and two metal Tonka trucks. That was the first time I had something stolen, and it really shocked me! Who would steal from a kid?

Perhaps someone might say having my toys stolen was a good experience. Life is rough. Take off the rose-colored glasses! Grow up! Learn to deal with it. Such comments make the child insecure and vulnerable.

My parents did their best to comfort me. They helped me to understand they were probably gone and there was no way to know who took them. They didn't have the money to replace them, but they had plenty of love to give me! Now, almost sixty years later, I fondly remember those toys. Is that such a bad thing? No, not really. My parents were right.

What things are gone but not forgotten in your life? An amazing thing has happened over the decades. I can't remember the exact details of the train set. Did the track have three rails? How many wheels did the engine use? What were the cars like? What about those Tonka trucks? I thought they were bigger! Every old train and Tonka truck I see aren't the same as mine. Were mine so rare? No. What is different today? I am!

> When I was a child, I talked like a child, I thought like a child, I reasoned like a child. When I became a man, I put childish ways behind me. Now we see but a poor reflection; then we shall see face to face. Now I know in part; then I shall know fully, even as I am fully known. (Paul in 1 Corinthians 13:11–12)

Why do we focus so much on physical things? Is Paul writing about a lost coin or a lost lamb? Does he recall a special toy? What is it that concerns Paul? Children are focused on themselves. It isn't selfishness; it's the only way of living that they understand. When Paul admits that he had been a child, he says he had been focused only on himself. He knew nothing about others. When Paul says he became a man, he is now equating adulthood with salvation.

God desires a personal relationship with us. He not only created us, but he also created the only way to achieve this goal. The plan he created was the sacrifice of our Lord Jesus Christ. When we accept Jesus as our Lord and Savior, our priorities change. Instead of a stolen toy, we should focus on lost souls.

I SEE JESUS

The day is coming when we will see Jesus face-to-face! However, our time is limited to reach the lost. Imagine the joy when someone tells the Lord how you helped them reach heaven!

A lost soul is worth far more than a lost toy.

(August 31, 2023)

Covered by the Blood

The air was filled with sound.
Some were hushed, some were loud.
There were screams of shame,
And there were screams of pain.

The sky itself seemed in turmoil,
Moving like water about to boil.
Black clouds crashed into each other.
The darkness tolerated no others.

Those watching were like the sky,
Some shouted curses while others cried.
None seemed to care about the two on each side,
It was the One in the center they eyed.

His own blood stained his hair red.
Thorns dug deeply into his head.
His shredded back had constant blood loss,
That flowed freely down that old Cross.

Each hand bled from a spike like nail.
His feet were also so impaled.
One thief mocked him to his face,
The other thief found Jesus's saving grace!

For three hours Jesus hung on that tree.
"Father, forgive them" was his plea.
Jesus chose to die at Calvary,
To bring salvation to you and me!

I SEE JESUS

Do we recall the spear on his side?
Do we ponder why Jesus died?
Believe me when I say,
Jesus Christ is alive today!

His precious blood was shed.
He was laid in a tomb: dead.
Then Jesus arose! God's Only Son!
Victory over sin and death was won!

The Cross and Grave could not keep God's Son!
Jesus is Lord! The work is done!
Jesus is our Lord and King!
To the Glory of God our praises we bring!

(September 22, 2023)

What about Me?

This world is such a rotten place.
People being mean is all I see.
No wonder we call it a rat race.
I don't care about them, what about me?

My work is always a pain.
Do this, do that, remember the committee.
Day after day, it's always the same.
Stress and pressure, what about me?

My wife and kids never stop!
All their texts are "me, me, me!"
I get home to hear, "let's go eat and shop!
With a sigh I think, what about me?

Church on Sunday is more of the same.
Everyone needs me! Where is Billy?
The sermon was long, should I say again?
Missed the big game. What about me?

The sun was getting low in the sky.
I couldn't take more, I needed sleep.
Then I heard a voice, I do not lie!
It clearly said, "What about me!"

I was instantly awake!
"My child, I died to set you free."
I fell to my knees and started to shake.
"Did you hear me ask you, what about me?"

I SEE JESUS

"I gave my blood at Calvary."
I crumbled at his feet.
"I arose from the grave in victory."
Why was everything all about me?

Please forgive me and save my soul!
No more will I live selfishly!
I have one life to give you Lord.
No more will I say, what about me!

Is your life a hassle like mine?
Jesus says, "Come to me."
Don't waste any more time!
Jesus is asking you, what about me?

(October 7, 2023)

The Real You

The people were different, yet still the same.
We all had our problems, sorrows and shame.
We put on a good show, masking the pain,
our counselor said, "nothing ventured, nothing gained."
When we left, we were still the same.

Many months had now passed, almost a year.
Some had joined us, some were gone.
Our leader would listen, but did he hear?
We shared our stories, how we were wrong.
Over and over, it was the same old song.

Suffice it to say, try as we might,
there had to be more, this just wasn't right.
You are the master of your own destiny.
Rely on yourself, you are what you think.
This cannot be right, that's what I think.

Our questions led us to a new thought.
Are we truly alone, must it always be me?
Then we found a faith-based ministry.
The leader spoke with authority,
About God's love, his Son Jesus and his Holy Spirit living in me.

Where had this Good News been?
A new hope was growing in our hearts.
Jesus is the answer for every sin.
Jesus gives us a new way of thinking.
Less of us and more of him!

I SEE JESUS

The years have gone by, and we have grown.
Jesus's love gives us victory.
His blood was shed for us at Calvary.
He rose to life from a borrowed tomb.
Jesus Christ is our Savior!

Do you have a life of struggle and pain?
Are you tired of things being the same?
God loves you and has given you the only way.
Jesus is the way, truth and life.
Right now, it's okay, ask Jesus into your life.

See for yourself, it really is true,
the change Jesus makes inside of you.
Sins are removed, habits are changed.
We long to learn more about God.
When you are a child of God, that's when you find the real you!

(December 10, 2022)

Why? Me!

On the sixth day of creation God created Adam.
God made him from the earth by using his own hands.
After that, God made Eve, and all was very good,
They lived in perfect harmony as God knew they should.

That was all long ago; today, what do we find?
Sin is running wild, Evil lives in the mind.
Jesus came to take our sin and give us liberty.
Why do we complain and always ask, "Why me"?

Trouble, temptations and trials plague everyone.
Even our Lord Jesus, God's only Son!
What is our burden that makes us complain to him?
Jesus took everything for everyone when he took our sin.

Jesus's back was whipped, his beard ripped off his face,
He was spat on, mocked, scorned and suffered disgrace.
He was smitten and afflicted, despised and rejected.
With his death and resurrection, we are accepted!

Let's be honest about our lives and the things we face.
When we ask Jesus to save us, "why me" becomes "Amazing Grace."
Have we had a spear thrust into our side?
Have we been nailed to a cross and left to die?

God gave us Jesus. He suffered more than you and me.
Jesus cried out, "Father, forgive them," not "Why me."
It's time to accept all that Jesus has done.
Let "why me" be changed into, "Why? Me!"

(December 16, 2022)

My Childhood Dentist

Take a trip with me back to the year 1963. I lived in a small town in central Pennsylvania. We had the normally expected amenities too. The barbershop kept the father-and-son team busy. The bank was the most impressive building in town. The courthouse was a remodeled store. The shoe-repair shop was our penny candy store. Downtown had two stoplights. We felt important because we had a movie theater and a JC Penney's!

My dentist conducted his business on the first floor of his house. I would take the steps to his porch. Opening the front door would hit the bell, making it ring. He had a part-time assistant. The waiting room used to be the living room. The receptionist worked in the former dining room. The door had been cut in half, so the top was open and the bottom half was closed. A piece of wood on the top of the bottom half was the shelf for signing paperwork.

To the left was a hallway for the rest of the house. The stairway for the second floor had a rope blocking access. The room directly across the hallway was the dental room. The dentist was an older gentleman who preferred the methods from his earlier years instead of the newer methods.

The only patient chair was to the left, facing the front of the house. Directly in front of the chair was his original drilling system. A large light was hung over the chair. This drilling system consisted of a steel cable that went over various pulleys to make the drill spin. It was powered by the dentist pumping it with his right foot, like an older sewing machine. The faster he moved his foot, the faster the drill would spin! He had a modern drill, but he said it would not work for my cavity.

I was ten at the dentist because my parents told me I was a big boy and could go by myself. I wanted to run out of that office! But I stayed. I had to prove that I could meet their expectations. After all, how bad could it get? Have you ever asked that question? Did it get worse for you? It did for me!

He put some cotton in my mouth. The water was running in the little sink to rinse my mouth. He was holding the old-fashioned drill. He was ready to start. I asked about getting something to numb my tooth. He replied that I didn't need it; it wouldn't hurt that much. The drill had a rounded end, not a narrow point. He managed to get the drill running at a slow pace. Instead of the high-pitched whining sound of a modern drill, it made a low rumbling sound.

Trust me when I say, it hurt. It hurt more than a fast drill. That was when he stopped and muttered something about the drill. He handed me a little push-button electric controller. He told me I had to keep the button pressed to keep the drill running! The pedal had broken, and that was his battery backup control.

The rest of my experience had me holding that button while the dentist slowly grounded out the cavity. After my tooth was filled, I got out of there as fast as possible. I never went back to him.

Though I did not realize it back then, I can appreciate the experience now. I was only ten, but I managed to act like an adult, even being a participant in my own procedure. Why did I do that? My parents expected me to come home with my tooth fixed. They placed their trust in me. Isn't that what Jesus does to us?

Have you ever thought that Jesus trusts you? He left you and me with the responsibility of sharing his love with others. Jesus is trusting us! He believes in us! He has given us everything we need to go into the world and witness about him. Even if we must hold a button and suffer pain, our Lord and Savior trusts that we will get the work done.

He has given us the Holy Spirit to help us when we truly need his help. This relationship is based upon our willingness to fulfill Jesus's expectations as he trusts us. Take a moment to think about your own lives. How has Jesus trusted you? Do you trust him?

> In God I trust; I will not be afraid. What
> can mere humans do to me?
>
> —Psalm 56:11 (CSB)

(October 20, 2023)

From the Old to the New

That's it! I've had enough! No more, I'm through!
I'm fed up! Don't say a word! Oh, what I wish I could do!
No! Just stop! Don't even try to say anything!
Just sit down and be quiet! I must think!

I sat there in stunned silence, what should I do?
He was so very angry. A man out of control.
I decided, while he was outside, to pray for my foe.
It was obvious, someone had to pray for his soul.

With my head bowed and without a spoken word,
I prayed silently, knowing my heart would be heard.
The more I prayed to understand him,
The more I knew Jesus would forgive his sin.

It is sin, deep within, that makes us act like him.
No matter how we try to hide it, others will know.
The struggle within the heart has just one way to win.
The sin must be given to Jesus, only he can make us whole!

Before you think badly of me; I used to be like him.
Loneliness, frustration, and anger boiled within.
I was harsh, judgmental and cruel to all.
My heart was cold, my soul without God, I had lost his Call.

One day the Lord Jesus found me; found me with his Love.
I knew his Blood was shed for me, on that old rugged cross.
Jesus came to me with Holy Power and Authority.
He saved my soul now and for eternity.

So, I humbly sought God's Mercy,
That my enemy would be my brother and friend.
The Jesus would reveal to him God's Majesty.
I wanted him to find peace and love, with Jesus his Friend.

When he returned, I sat quietly, waiting to see,
Would he be the same man, or a new man set free?
His smile reflected the joy in his eyes for me,
He grabbed me up in a huge hug and said to me:

My friend, what a fool I have been!
Imagine my surprise, while outside, I met the Lord!
I don't know how, but I know why; my friend, I met him!
All that I was is gone! Praise God for Jesus Christ his Holy Word!

(January 9, 2023)

In Him

"For in him we live and move and have our being,"
Paul declared to those in Athens.
He agreed that "we are his offspring,"
Let us believe and see what happens!

When we ask Jesus to be our Lord,
We discover what it means to live "in him."
The Bible becomes God's Living Word,
Showing Christ's love conquering sin!

Before we gave our hearts to Jesus,
We were confused, wondering what to do.
Jesus always loves and keeps us,
He encourages us to move!

Jesus does even more for us.
His Holy Spirit shapes our very being.
He prepares us to rise above earthly dust,
Adopted by God as his offspring!

Complete salvation is our destiny.
Jesus saves us and the Spirit sanctifies.
God's love is personal for you and me.
May God, Jesus, and the Holy Spirit be glorified!
(Acts 17:28 NIV)

(October 3, 2023)

My Visitor

The knocking on the door was right on time.
Why did he knock? Was the doorbell offline?
Could it be someone else? Did he bring the family?
My thoughts were like the house, things scattered wildly.

I opened the door with a forced smile on my face.
His smile was genuine, mine was a disgrace.
Come in, my friend! Please excuse the mess.
Always busy, busy, busy. I do my best.

My friend was so gracious, his smile sublime.
I am so glad to see you, it's been a long time.
Don't worry about the house, it's fine by me.
I'm not here to judge your home, I'm here to answer your plea.

His words were true, spoken with loving authority.
My legs felt weak, I had to sit, how could he know me?
How did he know that my heart looked like my home?
My head was pounding. When would he go? Leave me alone!

His voice was soft and soothing to my ears.
Let's sit down. You will feel better. I am here.
You knew I would come. I heard your call.
We have been apart too long. Your life has hit a wall.

I see scattered about, fear, self-pity and doubt.
I see dust balls of sin hidden throughout.
All the things you tried to hide are clearly seen.
I speak of your heart and soul. Do you want to be clean?

I SEE JESUS

I felt so ashamed. I just wanted to hide.
I looked into his eyes and started to cry.
With broken breath and a shattered heart,
I grabbed his nail-pierced hand. Yes, Jesus! It was you who died!

I give you me, just as I am, each and every mess.
Please move in with me, no longer just a guest!
Look in every room, every nook and cranny.
Look in the garage and shed, the basement and the attic.

Cleanse me, Jesus. I've had enough without you!
Please move in. You, and the Holy Spirit, too.
Then Jesus stood and pulled me to my feet.
He gave me a hug and spoke to me.

I will always love you and be with you.
I have taken your sins, now you are free.
The life I give to you is fresh, clean and new.
Hear my words, your life is now mine, your love for me!

My tears of sorrow became tears of joy!
My face lit up with my biggest smile.
My heart and soul were spotless and pure!
I give praise and honor to Jesus my Lord!

In the loving memory of Mary Diane Decker.
Today would have been our forty-eighth anniversary.

(December 28, 2022)

All We Need

God's love is for me, his love is all I need.
Love is my symphony; love is my Living King.
Love is my all in all, love is my daily call.
Love fills my very soul; God's love makes me whole!

Do you see God's love for me? His love alive inside of me?
Can you see inside of me? Do you see God's Glory?
My prayer is a simple one, that we see God's Son.
Jesus lives in my soul; seeing him is my goal!

Jesus won our salvation on the Cross of Calvary.
When it seemed all was lost, from that rugged Cross,
Jesus said, "It is finished," the war was won!
On that day Jesus took our sins away!

God sacrificed his Only Son; it was not done in vain.
On the third day God spoke up, Son the time has come!
Then Jesus rose from that tomb, alive for all to see.
His Glory shone like the sun, his is the victory!

Jesus is God's Living Love, our Savior, Lord and King!
Let him live in your heart; know the love he brings,
Jesus takes away our sin; his praises we sing.
God's Love is Jesus, and he is all we need!

(December 11, 2022)

My Thoughts:

Chapter 7

The Table

When Little Is Much

I was blessed as a child with four grandparents who really loved me. Grandma and Grandpa Decker lived in the same town. Their first names are a funny story. My grandpa's real name was Nathaniel, but he used Nathan. My grandma's name was Jennie, and her best friend was Jane. They decided as little girls that they liked each other's names, so they switched names! My grandma used Jane the rest of her life!

My grandpa Bennett's first name was Alfred. My grandma Bennett's name was Elsie. They lived in a small town over two hundred miles from our town. We would try to visit them twice a year. Since I could see Nathan and Jane every day, going to see Alfred and Elsie was a real treat.

Back in the 1960 decade, my mom wanted to take the newer four-lane highways to get back to her childhood home as soon as possible. My dad always wanted to take the old two-lane roads that meandered around farmland and went through every little town. You can guess which way we traveled. Eventually, we would get to Grandma's house. (By the way, why is it always Grandma's house?)

Every visit started the same way. After all of the initial hugs and kisses, Elsie would ask, "Are you hungry? Do you want a cookie?" Alfred would get off his easy chair and take me out to his little workshop. He would show me his latest project. Then we went into the basement of the house to look at all the stuff he had in there to work on or get organized to use some other day.

One day Grandma took me shopping at the local Woolworth store. I was somewhere around ten years old. She asked me if I wanted anything, and I said, "Not really." She held up a watch, but I said no, showing her my watch. Later, my mom took me aside and told me that I had hurt my grandma. She explained that my refusal to let her buy me a watch had hurt her feelings. That's when I started to cry. I had hurt my grandma. Mom told me to go and apologize. I went to her and told her how sorry I was about hurting her. We both cried, then we both laughed!

We laughed because we loved each other. Grandma hugged me with all her love squeezed into me. I hugged her tightly, not wanting to let go. That is the kind of hug I want to have with Jesus when we meet in heaven. I want to feel my Lord's total love squeezed into me while I never want to let go.

That day I learned a big lesson over a little thing. I learned to be sensitive to the feelings of others. Everyone faces a world that exalts violence and cruelty. A world where right is wrong, sin is acceptable, and everyone is expected to think and act the same.

Everyone needs and deserves the love of Jesus Christ. It is up to us to share his love. We share his love every time we share a hug or a kiss. When we take the time to explain to a child why something is wrong or dangerous. We share Christ's love when we empathize with others, when we are open and honest with others.

The Bible is full of people doing their best to help others. Our ultimate example is Jesus. He, literally, took our sins at Calvary and rose from the dead. He did it for us!

The other side of this means being able to say we are sorry. I mean, an honest, heartfelt sorry. People know when saying sorry is not sincere. It is far better to apologize and secure a strong relationship than it is to hold a grudge and destroy a relationship.

The next time someone wants to do something nice for me, I will graciously accept it and be grateful for their love. Until then, I will do my best to share my love with others as Jesus shares his love with me.

(March 11, 2023)

Gather Around

Hello, my friends, gather around; come and take a seat,
I have something to share, please pay
attention to what I must teach.
Do we ever pause to ask, what does a word mean to us?
Our word today, the one we study, is *trust*.

What do we think when we hear the word
trust? What does it mean?
Many people speak to us with very tempting words,
They tell us what to do while telling us, trust me.
We can't help but think, do we trust what we just heard?

Trust me is a common cry used often to deceive.
These ways of trust should make us question, where do they lead?
Beauty in the body, listening to deceptive words.
Extortion, the ruling class, and all those idols, too.
Forget about morality, mankind rules the earth,
Most of all trust in wealth and trust in yourself!

Listen, now. Hear what I say, the Bible is God's very Word,
With Jesus Christ leading the way, teach
us Lord, have your Voice heard.

Trust in the Lord, trust in his Precious Name.
Trust in his Light, he is our Stronghold for all time.
Trust that he is Eternal, trust in his unfailing love.
Jesus is our certainty, our assurance of Victory!

Trust is such a small word, that really means so much.
When all is said, when we depart, when all has been done,
Trust has no fear, it leads us to do good, and helps us to pray,
It is your choice, yours alone, to trust in Jesus, God's only Son.

(November 24, 2022)

Porches

There was a time when most buildings had a porch. A deck is a structure at the back of a house. I think most people have enjoyed decks. The porch is a whole different experience. So many modern houses don't have porches, and that is a definite loss to both social growth and personal growth. The following memories all come from living on a porch.

The first porch was a concrete slab in front of my grandma Bennett's house. It was six feet wide and ten feet long and one step up from the walk. Two decorative metal supports stood on the front corners to keep the roof in position. Flowering vines grew on the supports. A porch swing hung from the far end of the porch. There were no screens and no walls. If it rained, you got wet, or you went inside the house. A fly swatter was a prized possession. Bees were ignored, and wasps got killed.

This was a porch for family fun. While Grandma was always trying to feed us, we would talk and laugh and grow more in love with each other! From silly jokes to tall tales, laughter reigned supreme! People would wave while they drove past. Neighbors would stop by and join us for the fun! Calls would be made, and more relatives would arrive for the fun. Before you knew it, the kids were playing in the yard, and the screen door on the house was constantly squeaking with people going to and from the kitchen while Grandma was busily making lemonade and asking people if they were hungry. By the time things wound down, everyone was tired, but we had been filled to the brim with love!

My second porch was a wooden structure attached to the front of a house that my grandpa and grandma Decker rented. The porch was two feet above the walk. It had a small wooden railing and was four feet wide and six feet long. There was no roof, no screens. There was a glider and a rocking chair. My grandpa would sit on the porch to wave at people. He really enjoyed it when the elementary school across the street was done for the day. So many kids would hurry over to talk with "Pop Decker"! He loved those times!

He used the time to share in their lives the love of Jesus! Now that was what I call evangelism! What a wonderful heritage!

My third porch is located on Allegheny Street in Jersey Shore, Pennsylvania. This is an old two-story building with an upper and lower porch. Both porches were very large. I would say they measured ten feet by thirty feet with solid double-walled railing three feet tall. If people were sitting in a chair on the upper balcony, they could not be seen. This balcony was our porch. My parents and I would sit on the porch to cool down from the hot apartment.

We were next door to a creamery that had a small diner that sold ice cream cones and other frozen treats. I need to pause here and tell you a little bit about my dad. He loved to have fun. He was always ready with a joke. One day while driving to another town, we ended up in a line of army trucks. My dad was eating a banana while Mom drove the car. One truck had several soldiers in the open back. One of them saw Dad and motioned for a banana. My dad threw a banana, and the soldier caught it! So he ended up throwing all of them to the soldiers! They were laughing and hollering, and so were we!

One of my dad's favorite jokes was done on the porch. He would glance over the railing, watch someone take a bite of ice cream, then yell, "Ouch!" The person would look around wondering where the voice came from! Then he would wait and shout, "Give me a bite!" The poor person would look everywhere, in vain, for the speaker. We would sit up there and laugh!

Living in heaven will be like living on a porch. Imagine the constant joy and laughter! People who drop by to praise the Lord with you! Dad jokes that are funny! Everyone playing in the heavenly yard!

I wonder how the world would change if more houses had a porch? Until then, let us recognize that the Lord is Joy.

> At that time Jesus, *full of joy through the Holy Spirit*, said, "I praise you, Father, Lord of heaven and earth." (Luke 10:21)

I have told you this so that *my* joy may be *in* you and that your joy may be complete. (John 15:11)

The more we understand the Lord, the more joy will fill our lives. No porch? Sit on the front walk. Wave at the neighbors. The time spent in the front yard will be blessed!

(April 10, 2023)

From Stranger to Neighbor

(When I See a Stranger...You See a Neighbor)

Satan has worked long and hard,
To steal souls from the Love of God.
His methods are often subtle,
From false pleasures to incredible troubles.
All he does leads to one goal,
Deny God and Jesus of your precious soul!

Jesus is God's Living Word for you,
All he says and does is Holy and True.
A day of judgment will come to be,
Jesus will say, what you did for others you did for me.
Then the judgment will be given,
Eternity in Hell or in Heaven!

My friend, there is still time for you and me!
While we live on earth, and we still breathe!
It is our duty to touch others with God's Love.
Can we ever declare Jesus enough?
We must reach out to all we know,
And do our part to share Jesus with their souls!

Stranger or neighbor, which one are you?
Is it how you dress or what you do?
Does that determine if I should like you?
Should I write you off and say we're through?
Should I treat you the way of worldly men,
Or should I love you like Jesus, without end?

I SEE JESUS

Jesus is the example for us to see.
He lived to love us, he died to set us free.
He burst forth from the grave in victory,
To give us life for now and eternity.
Let us see each other as Jesus sees us.
My friend, we are very precious!

O Lord, open our eyes and hearts.
It's too late when the soul departs.
Now is the time for us to reach out,
Soften our hearts and remove any doubt.
Let us see others with your eyes of compassion,
Let us speak often and bravely of Jesus our Champion!

(September 1, 2023)

My True Family

I am the only child of my parents. For many, that would be considered a lonely experience. It would invoke images of a sad child sitting quietly in a corner. Trust me when I tell you, they would be absolutely, completely wrong!

My parents had been raised in homes where they were loved and cherished. My mom and dad each had two sisters and one brother. Being the only child meant I had all their love focused on me. Isn't that how Jesus loves you and me?

God is our Father. Jesus is not only our Savior, but he also considers himself to be our brother! "For whoever does the will of my Father in heaven is my brother and sister and mother" (Matthew 12:50), was Jesus's reply when told his family wanted to see him. Therefore, when we accept Jesus as our Savior, we become his family, making Jesus our brother!

Rest assured my childhood was not boring. I kept myself busy! I spent most of my time outside. I considered my activities to be an adventure while my parents wondered what type of trouble I would find that day.

There was a time when my dad would come home from work with a piece of candy or a small toy in his coat pocket. I would give him a hug, then he would let me get my treat from the pocket. My dad took the initiative to bring joy into my day!

God is the same way with us. He took the initiative to send Jesus to be our Lord and Savior. He wanted to give us his own Joy. A Joy that will be ours for eternity! We just need to reach into his pocket by confessing our sins and asking Jesus to forgive us. Then we can have the gift of Jesus's love and the Holy Spirit's blessings every day!

Finally, I remember the year I received a slot racing-car set with an electrified plastic track. The cars were six inches long, metal, with a connector that would fit into the slot in the track. That day my cousin and another friend had been invited by my parents to come and spend the night with me! What a wonderful surprise! We had a great time with lots of fun and laughter! This is one of my most cherished memories. I experienced what it was like to have siblings. I loved it!

I hope we understand what God is teaching us today. My parents knew that I needed to experience siblings. They made the arrangements so I could experience the blessing. *God knows exactly what we need, when we need it, and why we have that need.* He makes all the arrangements for us to experience his love and joy!

I am going to really enjoy being with everyone in heaven. Imagine the incredible family reunion! I want to run and jump. I want to laugh and rejoice in Jesus! I want to bow down before Jesus. I want to look into his marvelous eyes!

Heaven is my eternal home. Giving my heart to Jesus made me a new person. In heaven, I will be blessed with millions and millions of brothers and sisters! No longer will I be an only child!

Will you be my brother or sister?

Please give Jesus your sins and be a part of our eternal family! We love you!

(February 16, 2022)

A Parable

There was a farmer who loved the Lord.
He lived for Jesus and studied God's Word.
He was blessed by God with lots of land,
He decided to hire what he called a "helping hand."

Because he tried to live in Jesus's fashion,
His heart was filled with great compassion.
Soon there was a knocking on the door,
Four people wanting to be employed!

One person had lost an eye, another had one hand.
The third had lost a leg, the fourth couldn't hear.
The farmer just smiled; he had a plan.
Loving others like Jesus made them very dear!

The one without an eye was hired to manage the farm.
The one without a hand knew all about the land.
The one with the prosthetic leg kept the animals from harm.
The one who couldn't hear was the best cook he ever had!

God saw the love the farmer gave so freely.
He saw how the farmer helped the "needy."
He blessed the farmer beyond all measure,
God considered him to be a treasure!

Look beyond the surface to see the soul.
See others with God's eyes, if we dare.
What we see as loss, God sees as whole!
How we love is shown by how we care.

I SEE JESUS

Do we look beyond the obvious?
What do we really see?
Most people look to Jesus and see the Cross.
Look at the empty tomb and see his Victory!

Jesus is pleased when we love like he does,
When we see others as we see Jesus!
We owe everything to the Son of God!
Behold, our Lord! Only Jesus can save us!

(February 15, 2023)

Borrowed

This story is true. Emotions are a gift from God. Emotions add texture and fullness to our lives. This is a story about emotions.

Have you ever felt obligated to do something when you did not want to fulfill the obligation? If so, read on!

I was the pastor at a small church in a certain state. Diane was working part-time as a teacher, and she was also working on her crafting business. When I had the time, I would help around the house and help Diane with crafting. Since Sunday was very busy and the week was always busy, we made Saturday our day off. Yes, this was agreeable to the congregation.

Time passed with us enjoying our responsibilities during the week, then making plans for Saturday. We all know how life tends to move outside of our best made plans. Usually, when this happens, it is like a waterfall; everything seems to rush over the edge at the same time.

It was Friday night when an elderly member called us on the phone. There had been a death in her family. Would I mind going with her and her friend to a town about two hours away? Diane said it was all right with her. She would take our car to run errands. Her two stipulations were for me to be home in four hours and call her when we were heading home.

Saturday morning arrived with the two ladies. It also arrived with Diane wishing we had not agreed to my going with them. I was feeling the start of a very bad migraine headache. After a few minutes, I crawled into the back seat. This was the early days of cell phones when most of the country didn't have coverage. My headache was getting worse with every mile. I took my medicine, but it was very slow to take effect.

We arrived at the house, and I did my best to concentrate on the needs of the people instead of my migraine that wanted me to be physically ill. Everyone was very polite and grateful that I was with them. The time seemed to crawl for me. Could I call Diane? Would they let me use the phone? No, there wasn't time. Would I mind going to another house to see another person? Not at all, that would be fine. Off we went.

This visit took another hour. The time was passing faster for me because the headache was improving due to the medicine. I finally had a chance to call Diane. She was very concerned about me getting home. It was now over three hours. She wanted me home. I told her I would do my best to get home.

The women then told me we would make one more stop at another house. Another stop, another hour. The time arrived when they decided to head home. I was ready to go home. My headache was returning. A few minutes later, they decided they would get something to eat. What did I want? I finally told them they could get food, but my headache wouldn't let me eat. They made a quick stop for a hamburger. We finally started home.

Diane was angry, and I understood why. I was "borrowed" for almost seven hours. The day was over, and I had services the next day. Why was she angry? Have you ever been so worried about someone that you were angry with them? My dad found me one day after being on an adventure that nearly led to me into a whirlpool. He spanked me so hard that Mom had to scream at him to stop. A few minutes later, he was hugging me in tears and told me he was afraid he would find me dead. Those were very real emotions.

What were my emotions the day I was "borrowed"? How did they affect me? How were others affected by my emotions? Honestly, I felt trapped. My emotions led to my headache. No matter how bad I felt, I was determined to represent Jesus to the families we visited. The two ladies told me that everyone was glad to meet me and felt blessed that day.

Diane and I thoroughly enjoyed being with each other. We were not only married, but we also truly complemented each other. This was the main reason for our hidden emotions that day. Giving up our day together was an unusual event, which made it more acceptable to say yes to the ladies.

Being the pastor automatically meant I would agree to the trip. How is a pastor supposed to say no to those in grief? After all, doesn't the Lord expect the pastor to place the people first? What would the people say, or think, if the pastor refused? Should the people be concerned about the pastor and the families' emotions?

Yes, my emotions helped me to have a bad day. Diane too. When I got home, Diane was very upset. We spent a few moments practicing conflict resolution. Then we spent time talking about our feelings and how to move past that point in time. How is it with you? Do your emotions have a negative effect on you?

My friends, I have been very honest. I have learned to trust in Jesus with my emotional life. Perhaps it has come with age or a more focused life on Jesus. Perhaps the Holy Spirit is working in me. Trust me, I am always a work in progress.

I am thankful that God loves me enough to give me emotions and a Savior to teach me how to live with those emotions.

Remember this, my friends, you are never alone if you have a personal relationship with Jesus. He is always there for you, and me. His love is sufficient! My emotions are a blessing from God. In worship, in service, in fellowship and prayer, I rejoice in his holy name!

Praise God for my emotions!

(July 26, 2023)

I Want to Know

How can I understand God? How can I comprehend?
He who was, is, and is to come? He is Father, Spirit and Son.
He is three, yet he is One; he is eternal, without end,
Yet, he died on a cross only to rise again!
Help me, please, to believe. I really want to see Jesus!

Then I see the Holy Bible, often called God's Word,
I may not know how, but this I do know, the Bible is Divine.
I love to read and study God's Holy Word.
Then the mystery starts to make sense to me,
The more of me I give to God, the more I find that he is mine!

Jesus takes my failure and makes a victory.
The more I read the Bible, and the more I pray.
The more I understand, the more I comprehend.
What I don't know doesn't worry me,
Jesus will show me, when I am ready, all I need to see.

How is it with you, my newfound friend?
Do you struggle with questions, too?
If you don't mind, with your permission,
Let's change the focus and end the confusion,
Jesus is the answer for me and for you!

Give to Jesus your love, mind and soul.
Accept his forgiveness, he will make you whole.
Every failure and sin, Jesus will take,
Then rejoice in his love as a new you he makes!

(November 27, 2022)

Living My Dream

What comes to mind when we hear the word *dream*? The dictionary defines dream with fantasy, wish, hope, imagine, and vision.

Fantasy is closely associated with imagination. Many authors will take time to be alone to allow their minds time to ponder things they have experienced. This practice allows different thoughts to be considered for their books. Edgar Rice Burroughs based *Tarzan* on a real man who survived in the jungles of Africa for several years. On the other hand, H. G. Well's *War of the Worlds* was written as a social commentary.

Wish and hope are also closely related. They imply seeking a different future or a change in the current moment. How many people "wish upon a star"? Hasn't every child wished to grow up? How often do we hope for something to come true in our lives? Whether we use wish or hope, the desire of the heart is to experience a more pleasing life.

Vision is the final term to examine. *Vision* is the one word we immediately associate with the Bible. *Vision* is mentioned more than one hundred times in the Bible. Visions of God, heaven, and future events. Visions are used by God to help his believers. Jacob had a vision in a dream. He saw angels using a ladder to heaven. Jesus had a vision after his baptism when God spoke, and the Holy Spirit came upon him. John had the ultimate vision, which is called the Revelation.

Dreams were often used by God to communicate with people. He would deal with believers and nonbelievers through dreams. Pharaoh was not a believer, but God used his dreams to make Joseph the number-two man in Egypt.

Does God still work through dreams? Yes! If we examine dreams in the Bible, we might conclude that God makes them on a grand scale. Most of the dreams today are of a more personal nature. They may affect a small number of people more than entire nations or the history of the world.

This brings us back to how do we understand if a dream is from God or from our subconscious? The more we internalize events in our lives, the more we will experience dreams that make no sense, or dreams we call nightmares. Such dreams do not come from God. They come from our own minds trying to cope with everything in our lives.

I internalized lots of events when I was younger. I did not share how I felt about things happening in my life. I could feel the tension in my body. My mind was always reviewing events, even when I was doing other things. I was very good at not showing my turmoil.

However, I could not deal with everything that was on my mind. The tension was reaching the point of overwhelming me. What was bothering me? World peace? Politics? UFO sightings? No, nothing so dramatic. Most of my problems were mundane, daily problems. What was on my schedule after work? Did I have enough gas in the car? Was my wife having a good day? Daily problems and concerns make up most of our stressors.

God wants us to share everything with him. Literally everything. He wants us to be honest with him. This becomes a problem for most people because we have been taught to have respect for God. Respect is viewed as God is very busy, and we shouldn't bother him with our daily issues. Didn't he create us with the ability to make our own decisions? That whole viewpoint is wrong. God wants us to talk with him about every detail in our lives. Then God will reveal solutions and give us the ability to deal with those issues.

I don't remember the date or the year. I don't remember the town or the building where I lived. I don't remember the events that contributed to that night. I just remember the tension and turmoil in my mind and heart. I should say my body and soul. I fell asleep praying for God to help me. I confessed everything that had any possibility of being a sin or failure. It felt like Satan was trying to make me give up my salvation.

The dream found me standing at the entrance to a wide alley or a narrow street. The scene was gray and gloomy. A dark fog was drifting around the sides of the road. I could sense the evil hiding in the fog. My tension was growing and growing. In my dream, I kept praying in my thoughts, asking for Jesus to help me. I started to walk slowly into that road. Then, at the far end of the road, I could see the outline of a man. It was Jesus! I never saw his face. I never got close, never heard him speak, never got a hug. He was with me!

That was when I felt his incredible peace enter my body! His peace overwhelmed me! Every tension, pressure, stress, worry, fear was blasted away! I felt divine peace. There is no other way to describe what happened that night. It is impossible to forget such an experience! That meeting with Jesus was a dream with results in the real world. I immediately woke up, and I knew I had been visited by Jesus! His divine peace filled every part of my heart, mind, and soul!

Have you ever had a similar experience? Where do you find yourself in this story? When the time arrives, when you feel like Satan is working overtime to take your soul, would you seek out Jesus? Whenever I start to feel overwhelmed, I remember that dream; and Jesus's divine peace returns to my mind, heart, and soul.

I am living my dream. Thank you, Jesus!

(August 8, 2023)

A Tribute

One day the Lord revealed to me, in an unexpected way,
That he had me in mind for a ministry; starting today!
My first reaction was confusion. What was God doing?
I don't preach or teach, nor am I a missionary.
I love the Lord, so I say yes, but are you sure you wanted me?

I could have sworn that I heard Jesus laugh.
My child, I chose you because you are the best I have!
You see, I know your heart. We love one another.
You have compassion, sympathy, and love for everyone.
All you need to do for me is share the love I gave at Calvary.

Lord, it's you I love and obey. So, this thing you ask of me,
This form of service, my ministry; I say, here am I, send me!
Suddenly my heart and soul felt free! Joy arose inside of me.
A million questions faded away as trusting love overwhelmed me.
I have no greater praise than to serve my God and King!

When the times arrive with doubt and sorrow,
I think of Jesus and all he suffered on the cross.
He gave his very life so he could give life to me!
He rose from the tomb to give me victory in his loss.
Jesus's sorrow was the price paid for my tomorrow.

Everyone who will confess Jesus is Lord, and trust in him,
Will have their ministry, a ministry of love!
When we pray, or speak with compassion,
If we sympathize, or take time to listen:
We declare God's love. We are blessed in Jesus Christ!

This is my tribute to a very special friend in Christ.

(December 30, 2022)

Almost Perfect

What does it mean to be perfect? A thesaurus offers the following words for perfect: *ideal, whole, faultless, complete, absolute, finished, blameless, flawless, sinless, pure,* and *holy.* Does this sound like us? It does sound like Jesus!

Let's consider four people from the Bible: Mary Magdalene, Timothy, and the two thieves. We will examine these people instead of someone we might know. They can teach us much about our own lives.

Mary was from Magdala, an important city for trading located in Galilee. She had a very rough life. She was possessed by seven demons. She was a known prostitute. She probably used alcohol and drugs to ease her pain. She made many poor choices. Millions of people have had to deal with addictions. When people face problems, when events batter the emotions like a tornado, that is when sin whispers temptations into the mind of another victim. One moment of weakness is all it takes to suck the soul into the ever-deepening pit of sin. Mary Magdalene was so deep in the depths of sin that she was possessed by seven demons.

Have you ever felt so lost? Mary was found by Jesus, who led her into his divine salvation. Mary accepted his forgiveness and grace. How do we know that her life changed? She traveled with Jesus to support him and the disciples. She was at the cross, she was at the tomb, and she was the first person to see the risen Christ. *God's desire is the salvation of every person. Jesus is the only way of salvation. It doesn't matter what sin is found in our lives. Jesus will forgive if we just ask him!*

Do you think Mary had times of struggle after Jesus saved her? What occurrences act as triggers to tempt the believer back into sin? Is it true that the greater the sin, the greater the salvation? Is it true that salvation is the same regardless of the sin?

Timothy would be the opposite of Mary. His father was a Gentile, and his mother was a converted Jew. Her name was Eunice; and his grandmother, also a believer, was Lois. His family was well respected in Lystra. Timothy had been raised to believe in Jesus. He offered to work with Paul.

Timothy assisted Paul on his second and third missionary journeys, helped to keep several churches established in the faith, and went with Paul to Rome. Paul considered Timothy to be his "son" in Christ. Many people would conclude that Timothy had an easy life. We don't know much about his personal life.

Why are we examining Timothy? To show that God can use anyone who is willing to serve. Timothy was a young man well educated for life in their society and in service to the church. Does it matter to God our social standing in society? Does he consider our nationality or religious upbringing as eligibility for salvation?

Now we come to the two thieves. Luke 23:32–43 reports on this event. Both men were thieves. They had been convicted to death by crucifixion. They were men who failed to respect others. They were self-centered with little concern for others. One of them insulted Christ. The other man asked Jesus to forgive him. That man was told he would be with Jesus in Paradise that very day.

Why were they so different? The second man realized he was beside the Lord God! Do we recognize just how close we are to Jesus? Are we willing to admit our sins to Jesus? Do we desire total salvation? Let's be perfectly clear on salvation. Jesus Christ saves completely. A truly repentant person will ask Jesus to remove every sin. Jesus can forgive every sin!

We looked at four people. Three of them accepted the love and forgiveness of God through Jesus. Only one rejected Jesus.

Mary, Timothy, and the repentant thief. Before they accepted Jesus as Lord and Savior, were any of them perfect? Were they sinless, pure, and holy? Can anyone be perfect in, and of, themselves? No! All have sinned. If we could be sinless, pure, and holy by ourselves, why did Jesus go to Calvary?

The Holy Spirit is given to help us become perfect in Christ! Until we enter heaven, we will be imperfect people. We should always allow the Holy Spirit to lead us into being sinless, pure, and holy. Our efforts to live like Jesus will lead us ever closer to being perfect.

(August 9, 2023)

From Me to I Am

For far too many years I lived my life for me.
I loved my spouse and kids the same way I loved me.
Then I learned about Jesus, that even he loved me.
But his love was different, he loved me in spite of me!

The love of Jesus changed my life; from me to you.
No longer was it just about me, now it's all about you!
This is the truth God declares, I love you. Yes, you.
Respond to God, give him everything, give him you!

Just imagine what we can do, when me becomes us!
Me plus you equal we. God joins our we and we become us!
My me, and your me, equals we. A we is not an us.
God takes our we, adds himself, to turn we into us.

This may be hard to understand, one of God's mysteries.
But, when we look to God himself, what do we see?
God the Father, God the Son, God the Holy Spirit.
Our Creator, Savior and Sustainer, the Holy Trinity.

God's Name is "I Am," the same for the Spirit and Jesus, too.
Each of them is self-aware. A me, a me, and a me.
Yet the three together said, "Let us make man in our image!"
When we become one with God and each
other, we are more than us!

We become a child of God. We become God's family.
No more me. No more you. We are one in Christ the Lord.
The worldly self is changed by the blood of Jesus at Calvary.
The soul is freed of sin. Free to be fulfilled in God's "I Am"!

(December 25, 2022)

One Person

There are some very special people who have demonstrated the fruit of the Holy Spirit in their lives. They have a way of touching the lives of everyone they know. I am going to tell you about one person from my childhood. I will call her Martha, which is not her real name.

Martha was the kind of woman who could touch the lives of everyone she met. She was the traditionally typical grandmother type of that era. Her slowly tinting hair styled into curls. She always wore flowery patterned dresses. How did she affect others?

Let's turn to the Bible for her description: *"But the fruit of the Spirit is love, joy, peace, patience, kindness, goodness, faithfulness, gentleness and self-control. Against such things there is no law"* (Galatians 5:22–23).

Our examination of these verses will reveal how Martha touched many lives for Jesus and how we can do the same. Love is something God pours into us. We are born with love, but because of sin, that love is a worldly love. The world takes something that is pure and holy and corrupts it. When we accept Jesus as our Savior, sinful love is replaced with his divine love. God's love is clearly visible in the life of Christ. Once we have God's love in our lives, we experience joy.

Joy, in Greek, is defined as calm delight. Isn't that rather interesting? Don't we tend to think of joy as an emotional expression? It is fine to celebrate joy with our emotions. However, God offers us a deeper type of joy. Joy that brings us a calming delight in Jesus.

That leads us into peace. The peace God offers is not a political or a socially enforced peace. No treaty is involved. God's peace is from his heart to our hearts. God's peace means to join with him in oneness. That is far beyond any earthly peace.

Patience means moral strength. The more we grow in God, the stronger our moral strength will grow.

Kindness is based upon gentleness. This gentleness is not being weak or a pushover. It means having an excellent relationship with Jesus. Our Lord was never a pushover. Calvary was used to fulfill Scripture because Jesus allowed it to happen so he could willingly give up his life for our salvation.

Goodness is another attribute of God. It means to have virtue, to be beneficial. God is a virtuous, beneficial God. He has shown this part of his being in a multitude of ways. The most absolute proof is the sacrifice of Jesus.

Faith is the conscious decision to know that Jesus is our Savior and that God is our Father who is always the same. Knowing is more than a vague wish or a maybe hope; it is an internal absolute.

Gentleness is humility. Would we dare to tell God what to do? Do we know more than our Creator? Humility acknowledges the authority of God without seeking any recognition for itself.

Self-control means to keep away from sinfulness every minute of every day. It is a conscious decision to live for Jesus.

All of these make up just one fruit of the Spirit. Martha was such a person. Her relationship with Jesus enabled her to have a positive effect on hundreds of people.

People who met Martha knew there was something special about her. Every small child in our church crowded around her. Teenagers respected her and valued her wisdom. Adults cherished her while the senior citizens proudly claimed her as one of their own. After a building campaign, the church named the nursery in her honor.

My friends, may we grow in Jesus like Martha. How active is the fruit of the Spirit in us?

(August 22, 2023)

Let There Be Christ

God the Father, Spirit and Son; God the Holy Trinity,
You are three yet you are One, living in eternity.
You are the source of all life and love,
here on earth as in Heaven above.
Our God of creation, you do what you like,
The first words of creation were, "Let there be light!"

Lord, you are gracious, patient and kind;
yet often your words are a mystery.
I've been thinking, may I speak my mind?
Your words were meant spiritually.
Before the creation of all that would be,
before the earth, stars and sun,
You chose to make people who would be free,
To worship and adore you for what you had done.

You gave me freedom to think for myself,
you let me make my own choice;
You called forth the Light of Heaven,
the Holy Light of your only Son.
Jesus is separate from the darkness of sin;
he is the Light of Holy Glory,
Jesus is my Light of Salvation, my Lord, my God, forever my story.

Jesus is our true Light, in him we have our Life,
"Let there be Light," that was your cry;
To which I reply, let there be Christ!

(November 16, 2022)

My Thoughts:

Chapter 8

Prayer

A Talk with God

Uh, I'm not very good at this. God, hello? Are you there?
I, uh, I don't know what to do. Is this prayer?
Anyway, I was thinking about you. Just asking. Who are you?
I know, you are God, and that's fine, okay? Thank you.

My child, I am so glad to be with you today.
Just be open with me, I love to hear you pray.
I am your God, and I am your friend.
Share your heart with me for I am patient.

Dear God, I don't pray that much, just keeping in touch.
I went to church last Sunday. I even gave a tithe!
Anyway, the lecture, sorry, the sermon was tough,
It made me think about you and my life.

It's like this God, I will just admit it,
I've really tried to make things go right.
But things just happen; I know you get it.
I can't help it, it's out of control, it's a mess all right.

No, wait. What am I saying? I'm sorry, I lied.
It's all my mess, I am at fault, blame me.
I was wrong and too proud; I wished I had died.
Now there is no way out, no solution. Why, why me?

My Child, I am all you need. I am your answer.
My Son, Jesus Christ, wants to rescue you, right now.
Turn to him, give him your sins. His love is your answer.
He will walk with you every moment, day and hour.

With Jesus as your Savior, living in your heart,
Everything you do in his Name; you do for me!
My Holy Spirit I give to you. He will help you out.
He will teach and guide you, ever closer to me.

Together, we will conquer every problem,
Removing every sin makes your love grow strong.
We will always be with you; you are never alone.
Will you let us help you? Will your heart be my home?

Yes, God, yes, yes! Please enter my heart, come on in!
Jesus, I claim your sacrifice on that cross.
Oh, oh my! I can tell you are in my heart! Welcome!
Now I see that it was my sin that led to my loss.

Jesus, my Jesus, I love to say your name!
My heart and my mind have changed!
I must tell others! I am born again!
I am new, all is new; nothing old remains!

I praise Jesus! I adore my Lord and King!
God listened to me. His great love is for me!
Give God the Glory! Let our praises ring!
Jesus is Risen, he is Alive! Here he is, living in me!

True Growth

A new day has started, another new week.
It's Sunday, and God is the One we seek.
We go to church to worship our Lord.
The Holy Spirit teaches us about God's Word.
Our Pastors love and do so much for us.
They teach and sing and lead us to Jesus.
Yes, we are the church, that is true.
We do a lot, but there is much more to do!

Do we truly see the people around us?
Do we see their pain, sorrow, and loss?
Do we look beneath the masks that fool us?
Do we lift their names at the foot of the Cross?
Others need us to pray, so more will be saved.
Let us lift others to God's love.
His will be done on earth as in Heaven above.

As we lift each other up to Jesus,
God will move to save us!
Then God's power will burn in our hearts like a fire.
Saving the lost is our desire!
Our challenge, our calling, our ministry.
We not only pray, but we tell them, come and see!
Take them to Calvary, see the stone rolled away.
Let them see Jesus, only he can save!

The more we pray for each other, the saved and the lost,
The more we share God's love that Jesus shared at the Cross,
The church will grow, but attendance is not our goal.
Let us grow in Jesus's love. Our goal is another saved soul!

(December 13, 2022)

Living Dangerously

Sometimes the things we do for fun turn into events that cause problems. Only later, after our perspective has changed, are we able to see how God was watching over us. When I was a child, I had a tricycle, a scooter, and a bicycle.

From my perspective, each item was a blessing from my parents. I was so proud of each new item. I kept them clean and put them away when not in use. All those behaviors would impress my parents. They would thank the Lord that I was such a good son. Right?

No way! The real me, the truth about me, did not equal my imagination. I was "all boy." I was reckless and dangerous. I was good at not thinking. If they gave me a challenge, I would tackle it. If they gave me an opportunity to be stupid, then I would be stupid!

The tricycle age was very calm for my parents. Those years left very little room for adventure. My parents had no idea what the future would hold. If they knew the future, they would have kept me locked inside!

The adventures began with the scooter. This toy allowed the rider to move with one foot on the scooter while using the other foot to push yourself. It had two wheels and a handlebar for steering. Since there were no brakes, the rider had the option of dragging a foot on the ground or jumping off to stop.

Our apartment was beside a creamery. They made ice cream and various dairy products. They also sold their products in their diner. The only street for riding the scooter was next to the creamery. It was on a steep hill. The best rides started at the top of the hill. At the bottom of the hill was the main highway in town. It was very important to stop before reaching the bottom of the hill.

My solution was creatively stupid. I would turn to the left and zoom into the parking lot for the creamery! A stone-and-dirt parking lot. The one with tire ruts that had a drop-off to another lower parking lot. If I did it just right, I could stop safely. Usually, I went home with a new cut, bruise, or a banged-up toy.

The scooter was retired when I received my bicycle. It was my shiny, new ride. It had a mirror, a headlight, a rear reflector, a bell, a bulb-shaped horn, and plastic streamers in the handlebar. I added playing cards to the wheel spokes to make a slapping sound.

Our town had a small creek separating a park from houses. There were several small bridges over the creek. It was very easy to cross the bridge. What fun is it to use a bridge? It was more fun to pedal as fast as possible to jump over the creek! Oops! Missed! I hoped my parents would understand that nothing stays new forever.

Children don't understand budgets or stretching a paycheck. They don't understand the long hours of hard work it takes to buy a scooter or a bicycle. What they understand is the love they feel. As they grow, they remember the love more than the gift itself. My parents loved me even when they did not have presents to give me. The way they loved me was the way I loved them back. They loved me with the love of Jesus.

Sadly, there are parents and children who do not know how to love like Jesus. *Jesus loves us despite ourselves.* Jesus's love literally takes away our sins!

Did my parents get upset when I mistreated my toys? Absolutely! Did they choose to love me anyway? Absolutely! Do they still love me even though they are in heaven? Absolutely!

Do you have the ability and the opportunity to choose to love like Jesus? Absolutely! Is it possible for Jesus to remove your sins? Absolutely! Would you like to experience the love of Jesus now and forever? Absolutely!

Join me in prayer.

> Lord Jesus, I want to experience your absolute love. I give you, my sins. I claim you as my Savior. I love you! In Jesus's name, Amen.

We are eternally thankful for God's eternal love!

(September 16, 2023)

A Prayer

Precious Father, our Lord and God,
We humbly approach your throne.
On bended knee, to you we bow,
Only you are God; you alone.

You longed to show us love,
So that you we might know.
You gave us Jesus your Son,
And your Holy Ghost.

Here is our need,
We desire to do our best.
The work is hard, indeed,
By you we need blessed.

We are here to serve the Bride,
To prepare her for the Groom.
Please be our guide,
As we gather in this room.

Open our minds to you,
Blend our hearts as One.
Teach us what to do,
That your Will may be done!

May every program and activity,
Have for us but one goal.
May all we do please thee,
By the salvation of souls!

(March 13, 2023)

Sidelined No More

Yesterday, today, tomorrow; are the same to me.
Be it rain, snow, or sunshine I see.
If I am on dry land or adrift on the sea,
Day after day, after day, are the same to me.

I am the one by the wall at the prom.
I just feel like I don't belong.
I'm the subject of a sad song.
What did I do that was so wrong?

I stay clean, I always shower.
Yet, I get treated like a wallflower.
I need someone who has power,
Please help me at this very hour!

Don't be sad, I heard a voice say,
I was treated the very same way.
I shared with others every day.
But many just walked away.

My child, I have heard your cry.
It was for you I died!
I ask you to give me a try.
Forevermore, I am alive!

I am Jesus, your Lord.
I am God's Holy Word.
Yes, you are heard!
You can trust my words!

Deep inside I knew he was right.
My heart began to feel light.
My nerves weren't so tight.
Oh, what a marvelous sight!

Now I could see,
That God loved me!
I fell to my knees,
As I saw eternity!

What words could describe?
Jesus Christ is alive!
In him I thrive!
Salvation is mine!

You! And you! Yes, you, too!
I am new through and through!
No longer do people say, who are you.
I only want them to know you!

(August 19, 2023)

My Honest Prayer

Dear God, Father of us all,
Please hear me as I call.
I need to know what to do,
I need to hear from you.

I openly declare,
I am not scared.
I love you, Lord,
Reveal your Word!

I find myself confused,
This is old news.
People tell me what to do,
What about you?

Say yes, say no,
Stay here, just go.
Do this, do that,
We have your back.

Yes, dear God,
It is odd.
People often do,
Think they know more than you!

I will wait for you.
Your Word is faithful and true.
I will keep my focus on Jesus, your Son.
He is the Answer, the Only One!

(May 29, 2023)

Safety Bars

Sometimes God will use the most unexpected events or items to teach his children a truth. My life has been filled with such lessons. Most people have experienced such events without noticing them. Sometimes they are mundane. Sometimes they are funny. Regardless of the details, God's desire is for us to love him and live with him.

Every life is precious to our Creator. God understands when we might feel overwhelmed or unsure about events in our lives. Since he loves us, he is always finding ways to give us guidance.

Consider some of the parables told by Jesus.

There was a lady who lost a coin. She spent the whole day going through the entire house to find the coin. Then she went and thew a party! Isn't it unusual to use such a story? It was, but it wasn't. It was the perfect story for the moment. Jesus was teaching the value of salvation. The lost coin represented a lost soul. God will always search for the lost soul.

Consider the mustard-seed parable. A man took one mustard seed and planted it. If we had a neighbor plant one flower in the garden, wouldn't we think that was unusual? Jesus continued to say the seed grew into a great tree. The obvious lesson is, Jesus will bless those who willingly use the smallest faith to mature into a fruitful servant.

I will admit that I am an official member of the senior-adult classification. I still have a hard time with "Sir." I think that word should apply to real seniors. That age will always be ten years older than my current age. Anyway, I live in a place with safety rails, or grab bars, in the bathrooms. They are designed to add safety to the bathroom.

As we age, we become weaker and require more help. The physical body is a loaner. The soul is eternal and has an eternal destiny, which we are free to select. People who ask Jesus to be their Lord and confess their sins to him choose heaven. We are saved, but we still must accept the fact that our bodies will eventually stop working. This is where the safety-bars analogy may be used, like Jesus used parables.

Safety bars are meant to keep us safe; they are available to protect us from harm. Please open your Bible to John 17. We are going to highlight select passages from that chapter. Please read the entire chapter for context.

Jesus is praying to God about the believers after he returns to heaven.

> Holy Father, protect them by the power of your name—the name you gave me—so that they may be one as we are one. While I was with them, I protected them and kept them safe by that name you gave me. (John 17:11, 12)

> My prayer is not that you take them out of the world but that you protect them from the evil one. (John 17:15)

It is amazing how much Jesus loves us! Consider what is happening here: our Savior is asking God to protect us! Jesus, the Living Word of God, the Son of God, our Messiah, prays for us to our Holy Father! Wow!

If we feel like we need to grab a safety bar to avoid falling, shouldn't we feel the same way about grabbing on to Jesus?

Safety bars are static, bolted to the wall. If we miss the bar, we will fall. Jesus is not static. He was nailed to the Cross for our salvation. He took the first step! If we reach out for Jesus, we know that he will grab us even if we fail to grab him!

We could make an alphabetized listing of everything that tries to destroy our salvation, that tries to destroy our personal lives, that tries to turn our lives away from God and into despair and depression. Then we take that list and compare it line by line to the words Jesus prayed for us in John 17. How would they compare?

Jesus Christ is superior to everything on our list! Every problem or situation in our lives will never have the power or authority to override Jesus Christ! Jesus prayed for our safety. It is up to us to accept the love and safety offered by Jesus.

(January 16, 2023)

Take It Away

Here is my heart Lord, look deep inside.
Find all the things that I try to hide.
Take it away Lord, take it away. In your Love let me abide.
I am so tired of living a lie; it just isn't worth it, trying to hide.
I know I have failed you, hear my heart's cry.
Please be my Savior, in you, let me hide!

Take it away Lord, take it away; Take all my failures, all my sin.
They cannot stay, there is no room within.
Take it away Lord, take it away.
Lord, here is my heart, here is my soul.
Come live in me, come make me whole.
Alive in my life, this is no lie.
Life is worth living, when you live inside.

Alive in my life; in you I hide! Living for you, I am truly alive!
Someday I'll say, as I rise on High,
Take me away Lord, take me away!

(November 6, 2022)

Pray for Me

I love you, Lord. I know that you love me.
My life is yours for eternity.
Jesus is my Savior; he is my everything.
I give you, my heart. My soul to you I bring.

I have but one request, one thing I ask.
Serving you is my pleasure, not a task.
There are hard times when I lose my way. So, I ask someone to pray.

I need a prayer warrior to help me today.
One who is willing, who wants to pray.
Someone to encourage my daily walk.
One who is more than just talk.

Will you be that person for me? Will you bear the responsibility?
What I know and gratefully share,
your love and support is my prayer.

When you pray, whatever time of day,
lift me up to Jesus, send his love my way.
The more we pray for others, the more we find the joy of eternity!

Jesus prayed for us at Calvary. "Father, forgive them" was his plea.
Lord, please hear my prayer.
As I pray for others, may they pray for me!

(December 12, 2022)

My Thoughts:

_____

_____

_____

_____

_____

_____

_____

_____

_____

_____

_____

_____

_____

_____

_____

_____

_____

_____

_____

_____

_____

_____

Chapter 9

Witness

Testify!

Noah, Moses, Peter and Paul, giants of faith, one and all.
They inspire and teach us about the power of God.
Their faith and love helped to shape history.
They have great stories to tell; they do, but not me.

Me? My life is simple, mostly boring, honestly!
Day to day, it's always the same, just believe me.
Did I just hear you correctly, what did you say?
You want me to testify about Jesus today?

Yes, it's true, I love the Lord, that is no lie,
What would I say? My life is boring. I can't testify!
I may have a story or two, about Jesus and me.
Nothing about a great flood or parting a sea.

God has blessed me, along with my family.
We have been healed and kept in God's safety.
I guess God has done much to inspire,
My heart is grateful, my soul is on fire!

I want to tell you about Jesus, all he has done!
God took my shattered life and gave me his Son!
Jesus restored my soul and made me whole.
His story, in my life, must be told!

Listen to me, everyone, your stories you must tell.
Speak of Jesus every day; help to save a soul from Hell.
Whatever God has done, that is what you say.
Tell us about Jesus and you. Testify today!

(December 15, 2022)

Share Jesus

I love to serve Jesus every day.
His love is sufficient in every way.
In his Power and Glory, I will stay.
He is my Life, Truth and Way.

I am wrapped up in God's love.
My eternal home awaits me above.
When that day arrives for me,
I will live with him for eternity.

Your love I freely share.
Your Name I gladly bear.
The old me is laid aside,
In you I will forever abide!

Your perfect love cannot be hidden.
Your love is freely given!
Your saving grace I willingly share.
The love of Jesus Christ I declare!

(February 11, 2023)

Never Too Late

"I wish I had gotten in on this years ago," she said with an honesty that cut through decades of pain and strife.

We were sitting in a corner booth of a small-town diner. We had not seen each other for a year, so this was a very special time together. We quietly discussed everything and anything that popped into our minds. We told silly jokes, talked about construction projects, and an impending thunderstorm.

We talked about family life, from those who had passed to a newborn grandson. We shared our pasts and our dreams for the future.

That was the moment she made her statement. The quiet honesty of her heart touched my very soul. My heart was filled with love and rejoicing for her unexpected declaration. She continued to clarify how much time had been lost before she had asked Jesus to forgive her and save her. She was thinking of a lifetime of missed opportunities and lost blessings.

She had discovered that Jesus is always loving and compassionate, gracious and ever encouraging. When past moments arise in our minds to condemn us, we should see them as opportunities for spiritual growth with Jesus Christ's love. Jesus gave his life at Calvary, and he took his life back again at the empty tomb, not to condemn us but to save us from condemnation! Even now, Jesus continually represents us before God in heaven!

> There is now no condemnation for those who love God and are called according to His purposes. (Romans 8:1)

There was a softness in her voice. An honesty that many have experienced. Jesus wants us to believe in him. Some accept his love later in life. Although they might think, *What if I had believed sooner?*

Jesus encourages them to think, *Forget what-if, today calls me!* Today is the day of the Lord!

It was that excitement, that fire, I saw in her eyes. The desire to grow in her faith. The longing to study God's Word. The eagerness to be all that Jesus wants her to become.

Tomorrow is Saturday, her baptism day. She asked me to baptize her. I am honored and humbled to have this opportunity to be a part of her continued spiritual obedience and growth. Growing in Christ means having our heart, mind, soul, and spirit completely given to God, Jesus, and the Holy Spirit. When we ask Jesus to live in our lives, we are opening our lives to all three. It takes the Holy Trinity in our lives to accomplish our spiritual growth.

Only we know our personal relationship with God, Jesus, and the Holy Spirit. Do you know Jesus as your personal Savior? Just tell him you are sorry and ask him to forgive you. It's that easy!

To my precious friends and my sister in Christ, keep the passion alive and growing in your heart every day for Jesus! His love and blessings will be discovered daily, if you keep seeking his will for your life.

Be resolute. Be determined. Be loyal. This is what you can do.

Be obedient. Be listening. Be accepting. This is what you should do.

Be honest (with Jesus in prayer and in your life). Be rooted (in Jesus. He is the Vine). Be faithful (to Jesus. He is faithful to you!).

The baptism was done. She was buried with Christ, and she arose a new woman.

How do I know she is now a true daughter of God? She closed her eyes as she prayed from the depths of her soul, thanking and praising Jesus for her newly found love!

Together, every believer praises and worships our Lord and Savior Jesus Christ! To him be the glory and the power forever!

(September 9, 2023)

Eternal Love

Hallelujah and Amen! We are born again!
Jesus our Savior has taken our sin!
We are the ones who rejected him.
We nail him to the cross again and again.

Like those led out of Egypt into freedom,
We look back, away from God's Kingdom.
Thoughts of what once was,
Become the nails used at the Cross!

The more we entertain such thoughts,
The more we ponder things as loss,
The larger the gap grows to reach God,
The greater his Victory at the Cross!

Jesus Christ is greater than all our sin!
His saving grace is without end!
Jesus our Savior has taken our sin!
Hallelujah and Amen! We are born again!

(February 9, 2023)

The Question

How can I tell you about God? What do I say?
My life is like everyone else's. I live day to day.
I can tell by your eyes, it's very plain to see.
You wonder what has happened in my history.

I am not like Noah; Abraham is not me.
A man like Moses? That could never be!
Here is a summary, a short biography,
To see what Jesus has done for me.

When I was a child, I fell out of a car and almost died.
Or the time a truck hit me at a red light.
That day I was trying to swim and almost drowned,
Finally, the time liver cancer was found.

In every one of these, and in so much more,
Jesus was right there, with love and grace.
He gave me compassion, love and more,
Jesus saved my life, such amazing grace!

I challenge you, my friend, to review your life.
See the times with Jesus by your side.
Remember what he has done in your life.
Recall his endless love, how with you he daily abides.

No one lives an ordinary life,
When our extraordinary Lord gives us his life!
How can I *not* talk about God? Hear what I say!
Jesus lives in my heart. Is he in your heart today?

(January 7, 2023)

The Grace of God

Jesus is my Lord and Savior,
My Redeemer and my Friend.
Jesus is my Almighty Creator,
His love for me never ends!

Before I knew Jesus, I had no life.
Lost in myself, my soul was dead.
I tried to justify my sin with lies.
The Bible was closed, never read.

How my mind was locked tight!
My sins had become routine.
Then Jesus broke through with his Light;
He knew my sad state within.

God is so truly amazing to me.
He looked past my sin, into my heart.
God gave me Jesus to set me free.
Imagine it! The very Son of God!

Now I know about God's Grace.
When I lived for myself and not him.
God was working on my case.
Jesus was sacrificed to free me from sin!

I gladly give Jesus all of me,
My body, mind and soul.
All that I am and what I will be,
God has made me whole!

(February 24, 2023)

My Thoughts:

Chapter 10

Worship

What a Deal!

I must make a confession. I am going to reveal something that most people do not know about me. First, I wish to explain my childhood days. My parents lived most of their lives slightly above the lowest poverty level. Technically, we lived in poverty. My dad was raised during the Great Depression. Farmers would allow families like my dad's family to harvest crops. They were not paid. They were allowed to eat the harvest while working, but they could not take anything home.

My mom's family had enough money to be slightly above middle class. When Mom married Dad, she knew they would be poor. My mom loved my dad, so she accepted the change in her lifestyle. Mom kept a tight budget. Every week she would go to the fire station for free cheese and milk from the government. We never ate out, except for ice cream.

I was raised to be frugal, wise with money, to pick up pennies, that one bird in the hand is worth two in the bush. I was raised to be cheap. Don't worry, I am joking. I was raised to appreciate the value of the dollar. I like using coupons. I buy most items on sale. I appreciate a bargain.

I don't know many people who enjoy wasting money. People live with a limited income. People do, however, find ways to share their earnings. They share with the government by paying taxes. They make payments on vehicles, houses, furniture, medical care, and so much more.

God, in his love, made a bargain for our souls. He gave his only Son to take our place at Calvary. Jesus gave his blood to give us salvation. He not only laid down his life, but he also took it back up again! Jesus rose from the grave! He is our Living Lord! When we ask Jesus to forgive our sins, we become God's children. We inherit eternity with God. He asks that we serve him with all of our heart, soul, mind, and strength while loving others as ourselves.

Then God did something else for us, something that is meant to be a blessing. God established tithes and offerings. People gladly gave to the Lord. Over time, attitudes began to change. Tithes and offerings became a duty, then a requirement. People started to covet their own money. They decided God had enough money; others would give to God's church.

The word *tithe* means 10 percent, or one-tenth. For example, if you have ten pennies, and you give God one penny, then you have given a tithe. Let's look at two more examples: if you had ten dollars, one dollar would be a tithe. Two hundred dollars would be a tithe of twenty dollars. Is 10 percent too much?

An offering is any amount that we give in addition to the tithe. The only thing God asks for the offering is that it be given cheerfully.

In my book, tithing is the most basic step of faith. Giving an offering is the second basic step of faith. How hard can it be to give one penny to the Lord and then keep nine pennies for ourselves? Children freely give to the Lord. Shouldn't we be like them?

Remember, I, like you, need to stretch my income. When it comes to the Lord, I freely give to him. God loves a cheerful giver, and I love God. How much do you love God?

It is far better to give a tithe to the Lord than going out to a restaurant and spending forty to fifty dollars to eat. Everything the world offers will perish when Jesus returns. The only lasting treasure is what we give to the Lord. May we be people who value Jesus above anything of this earth!

There is an old saying, "Put your money where your mouth is." If we talk about Jesus, if we glorify God, if we seek to live a holy life with the power of the Holy Spirit, then we should put our money into God's hands.

If we trust our souls with God, then we should trust our money with God.

My friends, that is the best deal in eternity. Count me in.

(August 18, 2023)

My Holy Treasure

There is a part of me that I keep secure and hidden.
I keep it wrapped and protected, my secret pleasure.
Once in a while I check it, ready for use when bidden.
It is so precious to me, my very personal treasure.

My life goes on, hour after hour after hour, dull misery.
I smile at others, put on a good front, glad to meet you!
The stress of the day weighs me down, so I must see.
My hidden treasure, my selfish joy; safely secured, in all I do.

Why am I so unhappy? Why does my life seem empty?
I have a job, and friends, and a loving family
This I will share; I have my treasure inside of me.
It defines me, gives value to my soul; it is me!

Then, unexpectedly, Jesus said, *Come unto me.*
His words struck me like lightning, my soul was exposed.
What I had so well hidden was opened wide before me.
I bowed my head in shame, my treasure was no more.

Jesus lifted me up, to see eye to eye.
To him I confessed. Please take my old, rotted treasure.
I give you all of me! To you alone I cry!
I want Jesus Christ, alive in me, my Holy Treasure!

At that very moment my whole life was changed!
My well-protected treasure was worthless, too.
I gave my soul to Jesus, and he gave me his Love.
Jesus is my life. May I share my Divine Treasure with you?

(January 8, 2023)

Worthy Worship

We want to praise the Lord. We want to declare his Glory!
We want to share God's Love and tell Jesus's Holy Story.
Jesus is our Holy Lord, our One and Only Savior!
Jesus is God's Only Son, God's Word and our Creator.

Hallelujah, the choir sang. Hallelujah, Heaven sang!
Let all creation praise God with one voice! Let all rejoice!
Declare the Glory of God above! Tell of his amazing love!
Worship Father, Spirit, Son. The Holy Trinity, Three-in-One.

We worship you with our mind, heart and soul.
We give you our adoration! You make us whole.
We stand amazed at your Awesome Majesty!
We cherish you and seek your Divinity!

We worship you with our hands and feet.
Our hands are raised for you to use,
Our feet are ready to go with the Gospel News.
We join in harmonious worship of our Eternal King!

Let us join in a worship of purity and love to our Lord!
Let us worship God with a broken and contrite heart.
Let our praise be honest and worthy of our Lord.
We declare with all we are, *How Great Thou Art!*

(January 13, 2023)

Sing of Jesus

Sing of Jesus. Oh, sing of Jesus!
Sing of our Savior, King and Lord!
Sing of his Glory and Love for us,
Sing of Jesus forevermore!

Sing! Sing! Let our voices rise!
May our love grow to please the Lord!
His is the only true sacrifice.
Yes. Now alive! God's Holy Word!

Sing of Jesus. Oh, sing of Jesus!
He lived, and died, and lives again!
Sing of Jesus. Oh, sing of Jesus!
Only Jesus can forgive our sin!

Hear our voices! Hear our cry!
Our Master, our Shepherd, Jesus Christ!
You we confess. You gave us your life!
Of you we sing! You we glorify!

Sing! Oh, sing of his Might!
Sing of Jesus! Sing of his eternal love!
Sing all praise to our God of Life!
Sing of Jesus! Our Messiah and Christ!

(December 6, 2023)

We Will

We are here to praise the Lord.
We worship to uplift the soul.
Truth is in God's Holy Word.
Faith that helps to make us whole.

Our Father loves to hear us sing.
We worship whom we adore.
Sing out, make the rafters ring!
Praise him more and more!

Every day we will praise and adore you!
Every day we will serve and love you!

Let our hearts be light.
Let joy flow into our souls.
Our God is always right.
May his Light make us glow!

We give Jesus our adoration.
We live for him every day.
He is our only foundation.
He guides us in his Way.

Every day we will pray to you!
Every day we will worship you!

Sing hallelujah to the Lamb!
Lift his Name up to Glory!
Behold the Great I Am!
We will sing, holy, holy, holy!

I SEE JESUS

Let our voices be loud and clear.
Your love must be told!
We hold him so very dear.
Praise Jesus for saving our souls!

(August 10, 2023)

All I Need

Give me Jesus, is what I say.
Give me Jesus in every way.
Give me Jesus every day.
Give me Jesus, my hope and stay!

Jesus is alive for me.
He lives beyond eternity.
He always was, is, and will be.
My Savior for eternity!

Jesus gives me love each day.
He walks with me along the way.
He listens to what I say.
I praise him with my life today!

The Trinity is all I need.
The Holy Bible I daily read.
Praise the Father, Spirit and Son!
Jesus is risen, the victory is won!

(June 17, 2023)

The Rafters Ring!

The Lord loves music, he wants us to sing,
To raise our voices to Jesus our King.
Long ago, with hymnal in hand,
we would sing about the Promised Land,
We sang about Heaven, where Jesus now reigns,
of angels, cherubs, and all the saints.

Sweet Beulah Land, Paradise, and Glory Land, too.
Abraham's Bosom, the Promised Land, and marching to Zion,
And don't forget our Heavenly Home, and our New Jerusalem.

From a soloist to a massive choir, from one guitar to a full orchestra,
From a little child to the Heavenly Host,
God inhabits all the praises we sing.
From a slowly sung tune to a tempo with speed,
We sing to worship our Savior and King!

Be it a ballad or a whimsical tune,
Perhaps an opera, or a bluegrass toe-tapper,
It's the words that we sing with believing hearts,
Loving Jesus is what really matters!

Let the guitars play, let the drums roll,
Let everyone sing with the old piano.
It's the heart for Jesus that really sings,
It's our love for Jesus that makes the rafters ring!

(November 26, 2022)

Let Us Sing Glory!

Let us sing glory, as we tell the story,
Let us sing about our risen King.
Sing praises to our Holy Lord of Glory,
Our hearts and lives to Jesus we bring.

Jesus is our Creator, he made everything.
He rescued Noah from the great flood,
He led Abraham and Moses through everything,
And David sang about God's Love.

Then Jesus left Heaven to show us God's Love.
He gave his own life in place of our own,
His sacrifice leads us to life above
His blood on the cross leads to our true home.

Today we rejoice in the love of Jesus,
Today we sing praise to our Risen King.
Let us make sure in the way he sees us,
That our love is Jesus, of him we sing.

Let us sing glory, as we tell the story,
Our love story with Jesus our King,
He is Holy, well worth our glory
Our hearts to Jesus we bring!

(November 22, 2022)

His Story

This is the story of our Lord Jesus Christ.
He is greater than any other!
Jesus is our Hope and Light.
Our Savior and Divine Brother.

Jesus carried his cross to Calvary,
To give his life for you and me.
He carried more than a tree,
He carried the sins for all of humanity.

Jesus never sins, Pure and Holy is he!
His love has no beginning, there is no end.
Jesus always loves you and me!
Now is the time to begin.

Let now be the time your new life starts.
Give Jesus your love, and your sin.
He gives us a new life, a new heart.
Yes, Jesus! Please come in!

Here is my body and soul!
I give you complete control!
Take away every one of my sins!
I believe in you! Fully forgiven!

Now I know Jesus's love.
Why did I wait to believe?
Jesus is the way to God above.
Praise God! Jesus loves me!

(November 10, 2023)
(Port Bell, Kampala, Uganda)

Laughing All the Way

I was born into an extended family that loved humor and enjoyed humorous situations. God gave us the ability to appreciate laughter, to live a life filled with joy. I was born gullible. I provided many times of laughter for my parents. I wasn't embarrassed or ashamed. I always felt loved and valued. I learned that humor is a gift from God that helped to make me a positive person.

One day my dad told me eating watermelon seeds would make one grow inside of me. I believed him and removed every seed! I was fascinated with trailer trucks as a child. My parents enjoyed watching me as I tried to count the wheels. I wasn't old enough to understand there would be wheels on the opposite side. I was lost after I ran out of ten fingers!

Being a source of humor extended into the kitchen. My favorite cake was marble cake. I could not comprehend how the cake had blended white and chocolate!

Growing up with laughter helps a child to have a more balanced view of themselves and others. Children who are raised without humor will often experience depression, sadness, and loneliness.

God has made humor available everywhere. Sometimes humor can be found in the most unexpected places. My parents let me take our family car to drive two hundred miles to meet the parents of my future wife. I was very nervous waiting for them to open their front door. This would be our first meeting, and I was going to ask their permission to marry their oldest daughter, after we had two dates! I was trying too hard to act calmly, and that made me more nervous!

Her dad said gruffly, "You know we're Polish?"

"Yes, sir," was my nervous reply.

"Do you know how we got here?"

I was completely confused. What was going on? "No, sir."

"One guy swam over, and the rest walked behind him!"

What? Was he telling me a joke or testing me?

That was when he started to laugh. He was teasing me! That helped me to relax, and he started telling me a bunch of Polish jokes. Humor is available everywhere!

Luke 10:21 reads, "At that time Jesus, full of joy through the Holy Spirit, said, 'I praise you, Father, Lord of heaven and earth!'"

Then, in John 15:11, Jesus said, "I have told you this so that my joy may be in you and that your joy might be complete."

In these two verses, we find that God, Jesus, and the Holy Spirit are our living joy. Heaven is full of joy. Laughter is the overflowing expression of the Lord's joy living in our souls.

Our jokes, puns, humorous stories should be of a nature pleasing to God. The world's humor degrades the speaker and the hearer. Humor based on sin leads to more sin. Sinful humor is a mockery of everything holy. It is shameful, leading into the very depths of hell.

Here is a truth: Satan never laughs. Every mention of our enemy reveals that he is never satisfied. He is a liar. He knows his time is limited. It is impossible for him to laugh. There is no joy in his heart. He is the opposite of Jesus. He is not equal to Jesus. He chose to be opposed to Christ in every way possible.

Let us choose to be like Jesus! Let us live a life full of joy! Let us be known for our laughter! There *is* joy in the Lord!

(September 17, 2023)

Let There Be Joy

We have joy in our hearts,
We have joy in our souls.
We have joy when at home,
We have joy when we go.

Joy starts our day,
Joy lights our way.
Joy is our blessing,
Joy is why we sing!

We find joy when we pray,
We find joy every day.
We find joy on our knees,
We find joy at Calvary!

Jesus Christ is my Joy!
The Holy Spirit is my Joy!
My God is my Joy!
Heaven is eternal Joy!

Joy, joy, always more joy!
Marvelous, wonderful,
Life giving joy!

Heaven's joy overflows,
Filling our very souls!
When the trumpet sounds,
Our joy will be whole!

Give God the Glory!
Give him our souls!
He gives us his Joy!
Marvelous, Wonderful, Living Joy!

(April 7, 2023, Good Friday)

A Praise

We are here to praise the Lord.
Our worship will lift the soul!
Truths found in God's Holy Word,
Gives faith to make us whole.

Our Father loves to hear us sing.
We worship whom we adore!
Sing out! Make the rafters ring!
Praise him more and more!

Let our hearts be light.
Let joy flow into our souls.
Our God is always right.
May his light in us glow!

We give Jesus our adoration.
We live for him every day.
He is our only foundation.
He guides us in his Way.

Sing hallelujah to the Lamb!
Lift his Name in Glory!
Behold! The Great I Am!
Tell about his Grace and Glory!

Let the voices be loud and clear.
His Love must be told!
We hold him so very dear.
Praise Jesus for saving our souls!

(July 9, 2023)

My Thoughts:

Chapter 11

Christmas

My Revelation

It was just after midnight,
Why oh why, am I awake?
It was Christmas all right,
Was this real, or just a mistake?

I had been fast asleep,
When the cell phone startled me.
Being awake was incomplete,
My eyes slowly closed to reality.

Suddenly, I was awake.
A thought had ended my slumber.
What kind of day would I make,
This twenty-fifth of December?

Would it be one of gift giving,
Would love and laughter abound?
Or would I be left wondering,
Why are my bare feet on the ground?

My fuzzy thoughts grew clear.
This was the birthday of my King!
Jesus is the one I hold dear.
I owe him everything!

What a joy to think of Jesus my Lord!
Wonderful Counselor, Mighty God,
Everlasting Father, God's Holy Word,
Prince of Peace, the Christ of God!

Alpha and Omega, Author of Salvation,
I Aм, Immanuel, Man of Sorrows,
Good Shepherd, Our Consolation,
Creator, Rock, and Overseer of Souls!

My heart began to soar!
God's gift to me was his Only Son!
Awake all night but filled with joy!
Jesus's love left me overwhelmed!

God saw my life, the real me,
The life no one else could find.
I asked for his love; it was easy!
Jesus saved my soul and cleansed my mind.

Jesus has many titles and names,
I cherish each one!
My life is his, I'm no longer the same!
My life belongs to Jesus, God's Only Son!

(December 25, 2023)

Broken Again

Family and friends are coming soon, but what would they think?
No, not today, don't even ask, no, not even one drink!
How nice to see you! We kiss and hug, smiles abound,
We brought you a bottle of cheer; let's have a round!

We laughed and ate and sang about jingle bells.
As the liquid turned us into, what I dare not tell,
What did you say? How dare you! Get out! Get out!
Tempers were hot, the room a mess; how we did shout!

They left with curses and swearing, everyone heard.
We stumbled and staggered out to the curb,
Hot words were shouted, tempers on fire.
Don't come back! Some Christmas cheer!
Get out! Get lost! That was that.

The room was a big mess; yes, a lot of things were broken.
That's when we saw it, under the tree. Not a word was spoken.
We looked at each other, eyes filled with tears of sorrow,
What fools we had been today, but not tomorrow!

We fell to our knees, hand in hand.
It was at the Nativity that our eyes were fixed.
The figures were fine, except for one,
The baby to remind us of God's only Son.

Our hearts softened as we stared at the sight.
We asked Jesus to forgive us and change us that night.
The baby was cracked on the hands and feet,
Just like at Calvary; for you and me.

Will you humble your heart with me on bended knee?
Will you bow with me at Calvary?
Jesus is more than just a baby in a Nativity.
Jesus is our glorious, risen Savior and King!

(December 2, 2022)

Christmas Is...

Christmas trees touching the sky; turkey, stuffing and pumpkin pie.
Snowball fights out on the street; off to Grandma's for more to eat!
Socks and shirts every year, but the toys are what I hold dear.
Children and Christmas go together.
Each year gets better and better.

Every year as Christmas draws near,
my heart is filled with good cheer.
The toys were changed as I grew, into clothing, socks and shoes.
Sometime during the years of change, each year became the same.
Christmas was still a day of fun, but where had Jesus gone?

Christmas has changed for me, now I keep Jesus as my King!
Songs about elves and reindeer give way, to singing God's praise.
The more about Jesus I read, the more of Jesus I need.
Christmas celebrates his birth, when Jesus came to earth.

At Christmas we think about Jesus, only his blood can save us!
Christmas is the Virgin birth, and the first step to the Cross.
May Christians boldly declare, the love of Jesus everywhere!
Jesus came to save us from sin, now it's time to magnify him!

Why is there a Christmas? What are we to celebrate?
The giving of a store-bought thing, or
the story that the Angel's sing?
What is Christmas without Christ? Just an "X"-mas, not too nice.
The Babe whose called the Son of God,
deserves our glory, honor, and laud!

In loving memory of Mary Diane Decker
(December 22, 1954–September 13, 2017)

(December 22, 2022)

A Changed View

The morning had been wonderful confusion.
Wrapping paper and bows were tossed everywhere.
The children's toys were in every room.
We played and ate without a single care.

How long had I believed in such a fairy tale?
Your life is your life; but my life is hard.
I wanted a life where everything went well.
Instead, I ended up with a hardened heart.

My children don't live with me, it's not allowed!
They live with their grandparents.
Their mother resides in a jail.
Mistakes were made, the options were spent.

I know many who do not live "the dream,"
Many choices lead to a nightmare.
For many, reality is not what it would seem.
Worry, regrets and fear; claim life isn't fair.

Before you feel overwhelmed by all the loss,
Before you begin to doubt God's mighty love,
Let me, of all people, tell you about the Cross,
About Jesus Christ rejoicing in Heaven above!

I had been tossed aside by society.
I had been low and lost in deadly sin.
Jesus came to me and saw my need!
All because a friend opened my heart to him!

I SEE JESUS

I may, or may not, live the "dream."
Honestly, my friends, it doesn't bother me.
I only want to walk in the steps of my King.
When people look at me, may it be Jesus they see!

May they see the Holy Spirit helping me grow.
May they see Jesus, forgiving me again and again.
May they see God's Love washing me whiter than snow.
May they see the potential, not the "has been"!

Does your life seem like one struggle after another?
Jesus knows everything that seeks to destroy you.
Jesus knows you better than any other.
He died, and rose again, to forgive and restore you.

Are you willing to accept his sacrifice?
Are you ready to make Jesus your Lord and Savior?
Jesus is ready, right now, to give you a new life!
His desire is to love you, now and forever!

(December 28, 2023)

On Earth as in Heaven

Many stories have been started with "Once upon a time."
It might be a grand adventure or a silly nursery rhyme.
Some were flights of fantasy, and some were based on history.
They all had a story to tell, most dealing with morality.

This little story is presented for you to decide.
Is it fantasy or reality? I have nothing to hide.
Although my home is always busy, my joy is sublime.
My prayer is for you to have a home like mine.

It all started rather quietly, more like a feeling,
It was not a rumor, or gossip; never such a thing!
Something was happening, but what? I could not tell.
Then the Word revealed a mission for loyal Gabriel.

His message went first to a priest and his wife,
They were old but loved God; John would point to life.
Then he spoke to Mary and Joseph, her betrothed,
They would care for Jesus, God's Son, so they were told.

Then a host of angels joined Gabriel at Bethlehem.
The birth of Jesus was his message for all humans.
All praise and honor to God! Of him we sing!
Go and bow before the baby! Go and worship the King!

This may surprise you, but you really should know,
That message of God's Love amazed everyone at home!
I live with my family in Heaven; uncountable are we.
God's love for you and me is why Jesus went to Calvary!

I SEE JESUS

The Son of God, the Son of Man, the Sacrificial Lamb.
Jesus gave his life; Salvation was his plan.
His blood was shed to share his love with everyone.
He lives with me in Heaven; alive forever, God's only Son!

The incredible love of God is limitless.
His Love fills us and is his Greatness!
It's in his love we live and move and have our being.
I testify, this is truth, God's love is everything!

God's love is not a mystery, nor is it some story.
God's Love is Jesus Christ, for he is God's Glory!
I urge you to give your life to Jesus, God's only Son,
Join us in Heaven as we worship our Holy One!

(December 18, 2022)

Lifted Up

The shepherds knelt before the baby, safe in Mary's arms.
Tears of joy ran down their faces as they looked up to him.
Somehow, they knew, just not when, this newborn, God's Son,
Would be "lifted up" and save them from their sins!

Joseph knew the truth of God, his son he would protect.
How often he had carried Jesus on the journey to Egypt.
Joseph loved God's only Son, as if Jesus was his own son,
He would lift Jesus up and shield him in his own arms.

Joseph and Mary were aware of their responsibilities.
Their tiny baby, God's Son, growing in favor,
Every day they lifted Jesus up to God on their knees.
They cherished every moment, as Jesus grew from baby to Savior.

Three days ago, Jesus declared, he would be "lifted up."
That he would draw all men unto himself, at Calvary.
Now he hung on that Cross,
between Earth and Heaven, "lifted up."
With his last breath he won the victory!

Jesus was not done! Victory brings life!
Three days after Calvary, from the tomb he was "lifted up"!
Jesus is our Savior, our Holy Lord and King!
Now it falls on us, we who believe, to keep him "lifted up"!

"Lifted up" in our hearts and lives.
"Lifted up" in our prayers and faith.
Jesus depends on us to lift him up every day,
Jesus, we lift you up with our praise!

(December 24, 2022)

Celebrate and Rejoice

Come celebrate our Savior's birth, the Baby in a manger lay.
Rejoice, rejoice upon the earth, the Glory of Heaven is here today.
Rejoice, rejoice, sing his praise! The Son of God, the Son of man.
Born on this glorious day; the King of Heaven, the Holy Lamb.

The Angels sang from Heaven above.
Rejoice! Rejoice! Sing his Praise!
Sing out his Name, the Name of Love.
Jesus! Jesus! We sing your Praise!
Jesus! Jesus! Our Lord, Our Love! Jesus! Jesus! It's you we praise!
Jesus! Jesus! Our Lord, Our God! Jesus! Jesus! Above the grave!

Rejoice, rejoice, our Savior lives! Bow before our Glorious King!
Here is my heart, my soul I give. My very life to you I bring.
I celebrate my Savior's birth. Rejoice, rejoice, rejoice with me.
Jesus gives to me new birth, by giving his life at Calvary.

Rejoice! Rejoice! To him we give praise!
All glory and honor to him we raise!
He gives us new life, to him we give praise!
The Glory of Heaven is here today!

(November 9, 2022)

Behold Jesus!

Hear we now the angel's singing, glory to God! Our King has come!
Raise our voices in adoration to our Savior, God's own Son!
Peace on earth, good will to men, the angel's sing in holy voice,
Let us join this adoration, with the vast angelic chorus!

Come and see God's Holy Child lying in the manger.
Come and bow before our King; Jesus is our Savior!
Hear the choir of angel's sing, glory to God! Give Glory!
As we bow before Lord Jesus, we bow before God's Glory!

Tell the story of God's love; all praise must go to him.
How Jesus lived, and died, and rose, to save us from our sin.
His blood flowed down the cross, to exchange our sins for his love!
So, we might praise him with the angels in Heaven above!

Jesus knows our every sin, his love he does impart.
He will live, if we ask him, live within our hearts.
Once again, we hear the song; marching onward, ever on.
Moving on to higher ground, longing for our Heavenly Home.

There he is, see him now, his Glory beyond measure!
Jesus is alive in Heaven; his love is forever!
Come and join, we who believe, our lives are given to Jesus.
We love our Lord and Savior and praise the Name of Jesus!

(December 5, 2022)

My Thoughts:

Chapter 12

Heaven

Small-Town Fourth of July

Most of my childhood was spent in the small town of Jersey Shore, Pennsylvania. Usually, the population of the town and the surrounding areas averaged under ten thousand. The mayor lived in a house designed much like other houses. Our town had one theater, one barber, one shoe-repair shop and a Penny's store. Many children stopped at the shoe shop after school because they sold penny candy!

Another tradition every year was the preschool experience of the parents taking the children to Penny's for new clothes. Maybe our clothes were old, even threadbare. Why did we need new clothes? Blue jeans were stiff and always needed several washings to get softer. The washing process always turned the water blue, and everything else in the washer too! A lot of my shirts had a slightly bluish tint!

Children were pretty much "free range." Those were simple times with very little crime. Our policemen were very visible, so crime was very low. The police would see a group of us playing and just drive past. Our town was really into sports. There was an area near my apartment that was dedicated to sports. There were two football fields with a track for running. There were three baseball diamonds. Nearby was the town's public pool. There were tennis courts and basketball courts. The total area, including open fields and parking lots, was nearly ten acres. There was a small creek on the edge nearest the houses. Guess where we played? Yes, the creek!

There is another thing about living in a small town. We were very patriotic. All the things that people claim to divide us and isolate us didn't apply to my small town. Everyone either knew someone, worked with someone or married someone. The mayor's kids were my friends. The fire chief worked in the grocery store. He was well loved, and nobody cared that he was black. Nobody cared that I was white. Nobody cared that our junior-high geography teacher was over seven feet tall. We were all different. Yet we were all one small town.

As Peter said, "I now realize how true it is that God does not show favoritism" (Acts 10:34). Paul wrote, "The same Lord is Lord of all" (Romans 10:12).

I think it is time for Americans to be people who believe what Peter and Paul believed. It is time for people to reject those things that seek to divide us. It is time for Americans to drop the social and heritage qualifiers to boldly declare, "I am an American!"

I believe it is time for us, the believers, to reject everything that hinders our freedom to declare, "I am a Christian!" We must no longer submit to those who seek to destroy our salvation. We must obey the laws. We must pray for them. But we must never submit to them our salvation. We must "stand firm!"

Which brings me to our traditional July Fourth celebration. Our town was *the* place for July Fourth! One of the biggest carnivals would be there every year. All kinds of games were opened. Food trucks were everywhere. The many sports fields were being used to entertain the crowds. Vendors were lined up selling their homemade items. Every church and social organization had displays open. The fire company had their trucks available for children to ring the bell and pet the Dalmatian. People would drive from all over the state to attend our celebration. The parade on July Fourth was watched by thousands.

One year was very special to me. It was a day when my parents and grandparents were together on the ten-acre property. We heard the noise before we could see it. Then we spotted it! A helicopter! It started to get lower and lower, coming toward us! The pilot allowed time for the people to make a place for him to land. He landed smoothly and shut it down. What was going on? He had everyone's attention.

He hung a sign reading, "Rides $20.00 per person." Instantly, he had money in his hand and passengers in his helicopter. Off they went for a ten-minute ride over the town. This continued for a while. I really, really, really wanted to take a ride. I beggingly repeated myself. My parents did not have that much money to spend. I was completely crushed. I knew they were poor, so I accepted that I would not get a ride. Unknown to me, my grandparents gave the money to my mom.

I was still fascinated by the helicopter. After another landing the pilot told us, still a large group, that he would be leaving after this last flight. Then my dad approached the pilot, money in hand, and asked if I could go by myself! He wasn't allowed to fly due to a medical condition. The pilot said yes!

I couldn't believe what had just happened! I hugged and kissed everyone! The best part was I was placed in the copilot's seat! What an experience! Three other people rode in back. Once we were ready, we had a full ten minutes flying above the town.

I fell in love with flying that day. I was free! I wasn't sick. I wasn't afraid. I knew I could trust the pilot. I loved the feel of the air, the smell of the sky. I landed a different person. I thanked the pilot with my best smile and a handshake. I am sure I wore out my parents since I couldn't stop talking about my experience.

I kind of imagine going to heaven could be like my helicopter ride. The moment my soul leaves the body, an angel will take my hand.

"Are you ready to go?"

"Oh, yes! I love to fly!"

"You will be home soon."

Are we ready to fly home?

> Heaven rises over me,
> Homeward I go.
> Jesus I will see,
> Savior of my soul!

(April 16, 2023)

The Book

What do we know about the Book of Life?
What stories have we been told?
Will we read of victory or strife?
What is in that Book to behold?

The Bible speaks of many books,
From Moses, to David, the Prophets, too.
A page or scroll, forget the look.
Only our names inside will do.

What we call the Book of Life,
Is also called the Book of the Lamb.
Just as God keeps us alive,
God wrote the Book with his own hand.

Every name was in the Lamb's Book.
It was God's desire that all be saved.
Let us tremble when God reads that Book.
Dying in sin leads to names being erased!

Sinner's names will be erased from his Book.
Such is the last judgment all will face.
When God doesn't find us in that Book,
We will not experience his Holy Grace!

With a heavy heart God will say,
I wanted your love, my only desire.
But you wanted to live your own way,
Be gone! Join Satan in the Lake of Fire!

With the others, what does God see?
Names written in the Book of the Lamb!
God opens his arms; come unto me!
Welcome home to your Promised Land!

(October 6, 2023)

My Eternal Home

All people have a vision of Heaven,
Of the glories we will be given.
But there is more, so much more!
Come, let us explore!

Each entrance is made of a single pearl.
Wide open gates are never sealed.
There is no shadow, there is no night,
God's Son, Jesus, is the light!

The throne's of Jesus and God,
Are in the center of all.
The river of life, crystal clear,
Flows through our home so dear.

In the middle of the great street, the river flows past.
The street is pure gold, clear as glass.
The Tree of Life grows on each side,
Monthly bearing the fruit of life.

There is no temple in this holy place.
Instead, there is Jesus the Lord of Grace.
He gave his life at Calvary,
To rise from the grave in victory!

There we shall see our Savior's face.
We will see Love and Grace.
The intensity of his eyes seems like fire,
To worship Jesus is our desire!

I SEE JESUS

Jesus said, "Blessed are those who wash their robes,"
Washed in the Blood of the Lamb.
Our sins must be given to Jesus alone,
To spend eternity in that Heavenly Land!

Until the day God calls us home,
We must live and work for God above.
Forever with Jesus, never alone,
Born again by Jesus's Love!

Some may long for Heaven,
Some wait for New Jerusalem.
I long to live for Jesus, God's only Son.
Then hear him say to me, "Well done!"

(February 23, 2023)

Heaven's True Glory

I see beyond the starry sky, the great expanse of space.
I see the place where Jesus lives; Heaven is filled with God's Grace.
There I find all the redeemed,
those cleansed by the Blood of the Lamb.
They stretch on for eternity, Heaven must be an endless land.

Then from that great vast multitude, steps forth people I know.
They run to me with outstretched arms; their faces are aglow.
I see that they are perfect in every possible way.
We hug and kiss, we run and jump, like children at play.

How can I find words to describe the beauty around me?
The colors are greater and more vibrant than any ever seen.
The light of Jesus illuminates so much to discover,
His is the Perfect Light that lasts forever!

The sounds of Heaven are truly glorious.
Angels sing with the redeemed, millions and millions of voices.
Hear the voice of Jesus, hear the voice of God.
His is the sweetest voice, the most loving ever heard!

We learn about Heaven from Genesis to Revelation,
Our eternal home is beyond our imagination.
The beauty of our destiny will leave us in awe,
Our greatest joy will be meeting, in person, Jesus and God!

The Pure Glory of Jesus Christ we will see,
As we bow, as we fall, before his Majesty.
In his Divine Love, he lifts us, to look into our eyes,
The Creator and the created, now unified!

I SEE JESUS

In his eyes we see pure love, we are completely accepted.
In his eyes we see into the eyes of God.
Beyond the beauty, more than the Majesty.
God really does know me! My Father loves *Me*!

(December 17, 2022)

Well Done

Was this a dream?

He wasn't sure. The room seemed familiar in the hazy darkness. Was he sitting in a chair? The table was on the far side of the room. He could see the various dishes placed on the table. The question seemed to float into his thoughts, *Why is the table set?*

He slowly began to realize that he was in bed, leaning on the pillows with a cover over his legs. He was very confused. The room seemed familiar, or was it? The darkness was slightly fading, allowing him to see more details of the room. The few pieces of furniture were like old friends. He had used them for many years. They were well worn, but they were still solid, ready for many more years of service.

A gentle smile appeared on his face as he thought about service. Service. How much he enjoyed being able to help others. He had always been a man of service. Again, the room around him began to fade. He knew something was happening as an unexpected sense of calmness wrapped around his thoughts. He was relaxed, so very relaxed. Was this a dream? His eyes slowly closed.

"Dad! Dad!"

He jolted awake! He would know that boy's voice anywhere. He had just closed his eyes for a short nap. He had worked hard all day. He was doing very well with his business. He seemed to recall something about being a man of service. That was the moment he became aware of the sweet aroma of freshly baked bread. The meal was just about ready. He remembered his two sons were outside. He found them rolling around on the ground like small children.

"Stop!" His voice was firm and authoritative.

Simon and Joses jumped to their feet. They stood submissively with their heads down.

"Well?"

The question seemed to float between the two boys searching for an answer.

Simon spoke quietly. "Sir, we apologize for our actions."

He could feel his muscles relaxing.

Simon continued, "I must be honest with you. We never called you."

The words froze in his mind. Suddenly, he felt exhausted. Was this just a dream? He couldn't keep his eyes open. The darkness surrounded him again.

What was the smell? His eyes opened to see the face of a camel! Its breath was horrible! Why was he looking at a camel? Where was his donkey? Wait a moment! There were more camels! That was when he heard the voices coming from inside the house. Who were those men? He entered the house and found the wealthy men bowing down before his son! In front of his wife sat ornately decorated containers. He was going to say something when everything suddenly changed.

What was happening to him? He could see himself, his wife, and their newly born son. How could this be happening? His confusion started to increase. Was he losing his mind? How could he see himself? Was he dreaming?

He whispered, "Oh, please, let this be a dream!" He purposely closed his eyes.

His eyes opened as he heard a familiar voice. He thought of the time he had been visited by Gabriel. But, no, that was not his voice. Something was different. This voice was so rich, so full of love. It was soft, yet ultimately confident. He knew he was hearing the Father of his son. The sense of peace returned and overwhelmed him as he listened to God.

"Joseph of Nazareth!"

"Abba, I am here!"

"Joseph, I am very pleased with you. You have been a fine earthly dad for my son. You gave him the examples he needed to mature into a man. You have been the husband Mary needed. I have provided your needs for your family, and I will continue to provide for them. Now, my child, it is time for you to rest in my presence. I say to you, well done. You have been a good and faithful servant. Welcome home, Joseph."

The room was dark except for one candle. Mary, Jesus, and the other children surrounded Joseph's bed. Mary was holding Joseph's right hand. She gently held a cooling cloth on his brow. Tears silently slipped down her face. Jesus stood holding his left hand. The other children were standing around the bed, quietly weeping.

They all knew the moment of death had arrived. Jesus was now the leader of the family. Everyone looked at him. They were seeking his leadership, his guidance. They saw the tears on his face. Tears of loss but, somehow, tears of victory.

Jesus spoke softly but with an authority and confidence that surprised them. "Fear not, Joseph is with me. Now and forever."

His family obviously did not understand, but Mary pondered all these things in her heart.

(December 13, 2023)

See It Through

I have given my life to Jesus,
I have knelt in his Blood at the Cross.
I cried out for him to take my sin,
And make me new in him.

Jesus heard my heartfelt cry.
It is for you I die.
That was when my sins were banished.
Jesus said, "It is finished!"

He was gently laid in the tomb.
Everyone was filled with gloom.
Those were the longest hours.
We were his, but was he ours?

Can you imagine my rejoicing,
When Jesus arose, my Holy King?
His Glory is his Divine Love.
His throne is in Heaven above!

O Lord, I give you my life,
Joy and peace with my sorrow and strife.
All that I am I give to you.
What will you have me do?

Draw close to me, I heard him say.
Read my Word daily, most of all pray.
My Holy Spirit is yours; he will guide you.
He will open your future to you.

When you have failure, I support you.
When you have victory, I rejoice with you.
Rest assured; I am always with you.
I will help you get through!

I have a place for you with me.
Yes, Heaven you will see.
Until then, to me stay true.
See it through! See it through!

Say "no" to all doubt and fear.
Say "yes" to my love and cheer.
To you I am always true.
I will see you through because I love you!

(February 20, 2023)

My Thoughts:

Afterword

Better Late Than Never

It was September 2, 2023, a hot, humid Saturday. I was busy cleaning and organizing my apartment. While most people do spring cleaning, I managed to get started for late-summer cleaning. Better late than never.

Cleaning and organizing is a rather long project. First comes the part where I admit the place needs cleaning. For example, the layer of dust on the blades of the ceiling fan causes aerodynamic drag, raising the cost of the electric bill. The second step requires finding the cleaning tools and supplies. The hunt begins at home and is concluded at the store, buying items to replace the old things that frightened me when I found them.

The third step is visualizing my goal and how to achieve that goal. I decided to compartmentalize, a fancy word for placing items in plastic containers. I was hoping to avoid future scavenger hunts and owning five staple removers and four staplers.

My fourth step started chaos. Let's see, put this here and put that over there, then—no, wait—where did that come from? Okay, start over. But! If I switch things around, then where do I keep it? I need a break! So it went on for many days. It was a slow process. Better late than never.

September 13, 2017, was the day Diane went to live with Jesus. This makes September a very special month for me. Except for Jesus, Diane had the most profound influence on my life. We were married almost forty-three years. I knew her almost forty-five years.

In the late part of the 1980s, she started making all types of dolls. Not plastic or ceramic, handmade cloth bodies with dresses. She expanded into doorstop dolls using plastic bottles. She made pillowcase and mop dolls. The more she made, the more she sold. She had a marvelous talent. She sold over one thousand dolls. Which brings us back to September 2, 2023.

It was early morning when I drove past a yard sale that was closed. Normally, I wouldn't bother going back. While I was nearing the conclusion of my organization process, I realized that a certain size of furniture would fit in the area and increase my storage capacity. I recalled seeing a piece of furniture at that yard sale, so I decided to return and inspect the item.

I asked the man running the sale to remove the wheels and cobwebs while I browsed the various tables. On the last table, right in front of the pay table, was a doorstop doll made by Diane! I blurted out, "Oh, yes! One of Diane's dolls!" The guy watched me as I examined the doll and put it on his table. His expression indicated he wanted to know why I was so excited. I told him about Diane.

I offered to pay for the doll twice. Both times he said he was giving me the doll.

He said, "I won't let you pay for it. I have to give it to you to complete the circle. It has gone all the way around and has come back to you."

I left feeling blessed.

I believe the Lord led me to find that doll. It was in pristine shape, including the original hangtag. Have you ever found something that had been lost? Jesus told the parable of a woman who searched her house to find a lost coin. She was very happy after finding the coin!

Jesus sets the standard and example for us.

I believe Jesus led me to find that doll. Imagine the joy in heaven when we find a lost soul! Here is a hard truth: sometimes we need to get out of our comfort zone. We might need to go out and find a lost soul. We can't sit at home and wait for them to knock on our door. We need to go to them.

Be brave. Set aside fear. Ask God to lead you to just one person. Get to know that person. Spend time with them. Pray with and for them. Be a friend. Let them see the love of Jesus in you.

Remember, it's better late than never.

By the way, that doorstop doll I found is like my wife.

She is an angel.

(I will always love you, Diane.)

(September 3, 2023)

Welcome Home

He knew the sun was burning his skin.
The relentless heat was fire in his lungs.
His body was getting weak and thin.
He felt his life was almost done.

At least he was not alone.
Thousands were walking along.
They had started with great hope,
But it was burned away like smoke.

He was excited when the trip began.
Now he hated this barren land.
Everyone agreed with him,
Let's go back home again!

Moses had chosen God to serve.
His loyalty was sure.
Forty years in the desert did they abide.
Until that generation had died.

The truth here must be clear.
God will honor what we declare!
Do we complain about some imagined loss?
Or do we claim Jesus's victory at the cross?

Joshua told the people to declare,
Choose Satan or God, claim your share.
As for me, I will serve the Lord!
God is my Refuge, I obey his Word.

Yes, the choice is up to you.
Who will you trust to see you through?
The cross is stained with Jesus's Blood.
The tomb was conquered by his love!

Claim God's only Son as your own.
Accept forgiveness to be welcomed home!
Leave behind the desert of self and sin.
Welcome home, my child, come on in!

(See Matthew 6:21)
(February 14, 2023)

My Thoughts:

A man after God's own heart is the best description I can think of for my friend Al Decker. He is a man of integrity who loves God and others with all his heart. Al has written his first book which is filled with his personal life experiences and with God as his Lord and Savior. This is a book that you won't want to put down after you start reading it. It is so filled with encouragement and hope that you will want to read it again and again! It's also a book you'll want to share with others as well.

—Chuck McCoskey, recovery ministry director at South Creek Church of God and licensed clinical addictions counselor. He has helped hundreds of people into a relationship with Jesus.

*****

There are few people I have met in my life who have a more passionate and intimate relationship with Jesus than Al Decker. The thing that drives all of Al's life and ministry is a desire to know and make known Jesus to all he encounters. Whether it be through his words, prayers, or actions, you can count on Al to be ready to share the love of Jesus in a creative and authentic way.

—Reverend Aaron Perry, South Creek Church of God

About the Author

The Lord blessed Rev. Alfred L. Decker with a family that loved Jesus. His heritage is the Church of God (Anderson, Indiana), which goes back to the 1890 decade. He was raised to love and live for Jesus. His family deserves his honor. His pastors, from childhood to today, these shepherds, have helped him to grow in his faith.

His wife, Mary Diane Decker, managed to love and bless him more than everyone, except for Jesus, the Holy Spirit, and God.

In 2023, he turned seventy. He is busier now than when he was working. He spent ten years in pastoral ministry. Today he is involved at South Creek Church of God, and he is available for interim pastoring. He enjoys puzzles and painting. He especially enjoys socializing with fellow believers.

Above all else, he loves Jesus, God, and the Holy Spirit.